CRITICAL SECURITY, DEMOCRATISATION AND TELEVISION IN TAIWAN

Dedicated to the people of Taiwan

Democracy had been discussed in Taiwan as early as the 1950s, but replacing authoritarian rule with democracy was never inevitable.
- Myers & Wou (1998)

Other liberties are held under government, but the liberty of opinion keeps governments themselves in due subjection to their duties.
- Erskine's defence of Tom Paine (Keane, 1993)

Critical Security Series

Critical Security, Democratisation and Television in Taiwan

GARY D. RAWNSLEY
School of Politics, University of Nottingham
MING-YEH T. RAWNSLEY
Institute of Asia-Pacific Studies, University of Nottingham

Ashgate

Aldershot • Burlington USA • Singapore • Sydney

Published by
Ashgate Publishing Ltd
Gower House
Croft Road
Aldershot
Hants GU11 3HR
England

Ashgate Publishing Company
131 Main Street
Burlington, VT 05401-5600 USA

Ashgate website: http://www.ashgate.com

British Library Cataloguing in Publication Data
Rawnsley, Gary D.
  Critical security, democratisation and television in
  Taiwan. - (Critical security series)
  1.Television and politics - Taiwan 2.Democracy - Taiwan
  3.Taiwan - Politics and government - 1988-
  I.Title II.Rawnsley, Ming-Yeh T.
  384.5'54'0951249

Library of Congress Control Number: 2001087934

ISBN 0 7546 1217 1

Printed in Great Britain by
Antony Rowe Ltd, Chippenham, Wiltshire

Contents

Tables and Figures

Acknowledgements

We would like to take this opportunity to thank all those people who have helped in the preparation of this book. Our first and most important acknowledgement must be reserved for Neil Renwick, the series editor and a dear friend, who encouraged us to contribute this volume. We wish him well. We also thank the editorial staff of Ashgate Publishing and especially Kirstin Howgate for taking on this project and coping with several delays brought about by both authors experiencing repeated illness. We have found Ashgate a most agreeable publisher to work with – always courteous and responsive to our ideas. Thanks also to Professor David Culbert, editor of the *Historical Journal of Film, Radio and Television* for granting permission to revise for publication Gary Rawnsley's article *Popular Protest and the Media in Pre–Democratic Taiwan* (14:4), which appears here as Chapter 2.

We have had the good fortune of discussing our ideas with many people with similar, and sometimes not so similar, interests to our own. Several for reasons that will become obvious as you read this book have expressed a wish to remain anonymous, and we respect their decision. Those whose contribution we are happy to acknowledge include the following:

The School of Politics at the University of Nottingham, and the re-launched Institute of Asia–Pacific Studies under the wise leadership of our treasured friend and colleague, Professor Richard Aldrich; Professor Chen Wen–Chun, director of the Graduate Institute of Political Science at National Sun Yat–sen University, Kaohsiung, Taiwan. He and his staff made the authors very welcome during Gary Rawnsley's tenure as a visiting scholar in the summer of 2000, and were more than willing to discuss our research with us. Professor Feng Chien–san of the Department of Radio and Television, National Chengchi University, Taipei, has been a constant source of inspiration, information, criticism and warm friendship. Likewise James Tu of the *China Times* who was always prepared to meet us on our frequent journeys to Taipei and discuss Taiwan's media from a practitioner's perspective. We also acknowledge the help of sources at *China Times* and *Formosa Television* who have requested anonymity because they provided an insight into the KMT government's wiretapping and surveillance of journalists. Lu Ching–wen, Wang Hsiao–hsiang, and the DPP Legislators' United Office also deserve our gratitude for providing us with an extraordinary amount of material. Professor Lee Wen–ruey has also provided encouragement, assistance, and above all, friendship. Professor John Copper of Rhodes College, Dr Steve Tsang of St. Antony's College, Oxford, and Professor Thomas Gold of the University of California, Berkeley have been a source of inspiration, advice and information.

We also need to say a special thank you to our friend Joe Shiao for responding to our constant cries of help when things went wrong with our computer; and of course we owe his wife Monica, and daughter Jie-yuin, a special debt of gratitude for allowing him to spend so much time in our home at all hours of the day and night!

On a more personal level we express our gratitude to Tsai Sheng–hong and Shih Tsai–chin, Ming–Yeh Rawnsley's loving parents and Gary Rawnsley's tolerant and generous parents–in–law who always provide a home from home for us in Kaohsiung. Similarly Ming–Yeh's brother, Tsai Chung–lian and his wife, Lee Huey–dong for giving us the run of their apartment in Taipei. Ming–Yeh's sister, Tsai Ming–chuan, her husband Sun Xian–nan, and their daughter, Sun Pei–ling have provided companionship and many happy moments during our visits to Taiwan. Both authors also send their love and thanks to Jack and Shirley Rawnsley, Gary's parents in Bradford, for just being there when we need them.

Finally, to the legions of friends in Taiwan and Nottingham who may not have had a direct input into this project but have nevertheless helped to keep us sane during its writing, we thank you all.

List of Abbreviations

AP	Associated Press
APEC	Asia–Pacific Economic Committee
ASEAN	Association of South East Asian Nations
BBC	British Broadcasting Corporation
BCC	Broadcasting Corporation of China
BDF	Broadcasting Development Fund
CATV	Common Antennas Television
CBS	Central Broadcasting System
CCP	Chinese Communist Party
CCTV	Chinese Central Television
CNA	Central News Agency
CNN	Cable News Network
CPTV	Chinese Public Television
CSBC	Cheng Sheng Broadcasting Corporation
CSCE	Conference on Security and Cooperation in Europe
CTS	Chinese Television Station
CTV	Chinese Television Company
DCA	Department of Cultural Affairs (KMT)
DPP	Democratic Progressive Party
DPU	Democratic Progressive Television Union
FTC	Formosa Television Corporation
GATT	General Agreement on Tariffs and Trade
GIO	Government Information Office
ITU	International Telecommunications Union
KMT	Kuomintang
MMD	Multi–channel Multi–point Distribution System
NWIO	New World Information Order
PRC	People's Republic of China
PSB	Public Service Broadcasting
PTOC	Public Television Organising Committee
PTS	Public Television Station
PUTV	People's United Television
ROC	Republic of China on Taiwan
TGC	Taiwan Garrison Command
TMD	Theatre Missile Defence
TTV	Taiwan Television Enterprise
UN	United Nations

UNESCO United Nations Education, Scientific and Cultural Organisation
US   United States of America
USSR   Union of Soviet Socialist Republics

Introduction

'Security is what we make it'
– Ken Booth (Krause & Williams, 1997).

'One person's desirable social control is another person's denial of freedom'
– Denis McQuail,(1987).

Threats to security materialise in many guises.

On 21 September 1999, Taiwan was shaken by its biggest earthquake since 1935. The death toll topped 21,000, with more than 8,700 injured and a further 100,000 made homeless. Over 11,000 aftershocks made rescue efforts difficult and dangerous, and frightened thousands of survivors from returning to their homes. The cost of coping with the earthquake and rebuilding has been estimated at more than US$3 billion. On 25 September, President Lee Teng–hui approved emergency decrees designed to cut through bureaucratic red tape and expedite reconstruction efforts. Few wanted to politicise the disaster – it brought to an abrupt halt the increasingly savage Presidential election campaign – but many commentators found the proposed date for the end of the emergency measures, 24 March 2000, a little disturbing: The next Presidential election was scheduled for 18 March. Taiwan's English language press carried such headlines as 'Opposition jittery over rumoured term extension for Lee', describing fears that the election might be postponed (*Taipei Times*, 7 October 1999). Although only a rumour that was immediately denied by the Presidential office, this nevertheless illustrates how politics can be a cruel and insensitive intrusion at such difficult times. Some expressed unease with the potential for 'human rights violations behind the shield of the emergency decrees', and noted that the penalties for violating the temporary laws could be more severe than the usual punishments dispensed for robbery, extortion or assault (*Taipei Times*, 7 October 1999). The Legislature had no powers to restrict or review the emergency decrees. Others were more concerned that the decrees might allow the Kuomintang party (KMT) to increase its resources and, via the distribution of funds, expand the party's relationship with local factions ahead of the 2000 election: 'It's a shameless way of expanding administrative power, or even worse, a way of encouraging corruption,' claimed one opposition member of Taiwan's parliament, the Legislative Yuan (*Taipei Times*, 15 October 1999). Indeed, in the two months following the earthquake newspapers

1

filed report after report that 'discovered' the connection between the government's reconstruction efforts and political corruption, especially in buying the support of local factions.[1]

In contrast, media coverage of the earthquake found itself the subject of close political scrutiny. President Lee praised the way the three oldest television networks, TTV, CTS and CTV, reported the earthquake, and singled out the latter as particularly impressive. Lee urged more people to depend on the 'impartial' and 'balanced' coverage offered by CTV. On the other hand the cable news channel, TVBS, attracted critical attention, was accused of biased reporting and attacked for having questioned the government's organisation of rescue efforts. More disturbing were rumours that the director–general of the Government Information Office (GIO) had instructed the electronic media to broadcast government policies and information, a tacit manoeuvre to pressure the media into becoming more co–operative with the government. The media resented this, having spent the last fifty years fighting to rid themselves of such political responsibility. Li Tao, a TVBS talk–show host, responded by reminding Taiwan that, 'As a journalist or as an ordinary citizen, I have the right to say what I want to say'. That is democracy; the media had struggled for such freedom of speech through five decades of martial law. None were now prepared to back–track and thus jeopardise the consolidation of democracy. After all, the media had been a vital source of information at a crucial time: The deputy director–general of the island's disaster management authority recalled that 'The media was a great help. When the quake paralyzed the normal functions of a number of [government] agencies, we didn't know where to pursue life–saving operations until the media identified which stricken areas were emergency zones' (*Taipei Times*, 23 October 1999).

During the APEC summit in New Zealand, convened just two weeks before the earthquake, Taiwan's press were denied the opportunity to fulfil their democratic responsibilities – not by their own government, using its paranoia about internal subversion and communist threats to censor the media under a draconian martial law. Neither were the press silenced by the representative from the People's Republic of China (PRC), incensed by the media from the 'renegade province of Taiwan'. Rather, the hostility emanated from the host nation's Foreign Minister, Dan McKinnon. Facing a barrage of questions that sought an explanation why Taiwan was prevented from joining the World Trade Organisation, McKinnon replied: 'I have been to nine APEC meetings, and they are becoming more and more dominated by journalists from Chinese Taipei. We don't need a constant run of questions from Chinese Taipei' (*Taipei Times*, 11 September 1999). In addition to the obvious issue of the press being denied a voice, this also raises the problems of security and sovereignty: accepting the name 'Chinese Taipei' is the only way that the Republic of China (ROC) on Taiwan can enter many multilateral organisations and forums, including the ostensibly apolitical Olympic Committee. 'Chinese Taipei' is not a sovereign nation–state, and so its journalists should not expect the same basic rights and privileges as other members. How the international community views Taiwan can itself affect its security.

As the *Economist* (1 October 1999) affirmed, the earthquake was a 'brutal reminder' that Taiwan faces 'dangers other than Chinese revanchism'. Nevertheless, rarely does an event in Taiwan escape the attention of Beijing. The PRC announced to the world that the earthquake had occurred in 'Taiwan province of China', and the Secretary–General of the United Nations, Kofi Anan, offered his condolences to the same. The UN was required to obtain Beijing's permission before sending relief and rescue teams to the island. In the end, the UN merely dispatched two observers to monitor the unilateral efforts of a global response that involved 21 countries. China even refused to allow a Russian rescue team to fly through its airspace, thus delaying their arrival in Taiwan by twelve crucial hours.

Just a week later the PRC celebrated the 50th anniversary of the Communist revolution at an estimated cost of US$4 billion. This was in stark contrast to the mere US$100,000 in cash and US$60,000 worth of relief goods that Beijing donated to Taiwan. The Chinese Foreign Minister, Tang Jiaxuan, told the UN General Assembly: 'Our brethren across the Strait are linked together like flesh and blood. The plight and pain of our Taiwanese brethren move the hearts of all Chinese people' (*Taipei Times*, 1 October 1999). The discrepancy between rhetoric and action did not go unnoticed by the victims of the earthquake. The Chinese Premier, Zhu Rongji, stunned the world by claiming that the United States had 'emboldened' Taiwan's President and was 'making war inevitable'. Zhu declared that 'Sooner or later it will lead to an armed resolution of the question because the Chinese people will become impatient'. An audience member at the Fortune Global Forum that brings together some of the biggest corporate names from the US and elsewhere, said:

> ... Zhu went into a long and somewhat passionate tirade about Taiwan and he said the US has to quit emphasising that it must be settled by peaceful means and implying that it would help to defend Taiwan *(Taipei Times*, 1 October 1999).

It is not surprising, therefore, that even the earthquake could not pause debate on Taiwan's proposed involvement in the US–led Theatre Missile Defence (TMD) system, a project many believed would:

> ensure the stability and security of the Taiwan Strait, ... set up a close integration with the strategic structures of key countries in the Asia–Pacific region – especially Japan and the US – and ... establish a quasi–military alliance and security community (*Taipei Times*, 31 August 1999).

In the rush to praise a missile defence system designed to provide 'an effective deterrent against any reckless move by China ...', few misgivings were heard. China's unsurprising opposition to Taiwan's inclusion in TMD was dismissed as bombast; nobody questioned whether TMD might actually escalate the regional arms race in the way the American Strategic Defence Initiative had destroyed the delicate superpower balance in the early 1980s.

Taiwan and Security

> *'We have to admit that the greatest evils which oppress civilized nations are the result of war – not so much of actual wars in the past or present as of the unremitting, indeed ever–increasing preparation for war in the future'* (Kant in Reiss, 1991).

The choice of Taiwan as our focus of inquiry must be justified. After all, any one of the political systems involved in the so–called Third Wave of democratisation could serve as a useful case–study of the relationship between the media and security. What makes Taiwan so exceptional? The most interesting, though also certainly the most frustrating reason is that Taiwan does not lend itself to analysis by the application of a single theory or model. Taiwan represents one of the most complex and atypical transitions from authoritarianism. It was certainly one of the smoothest, least confrontational, most inclusive, and somewhat successful transitions that serves as a comparison to the disarray of democratisation in other areas. Its complexity therefore challenges the more pedestrian and effortless approaches to security that tarnish much of the literature. As the following will suggest, Taiwan defies simple explanation by a single model, realist or post–modern.

We can also view on Taiwan evidence for the fashionable notion that democracy and security are not necessarily analogous. In fact several of the more trenchant critics have argued that democratisation has in fact made Taiwan *less* secure than previously. Not only has pluralism encouraged greater competition between interest groups and parties, and thus a sense that political discourse has been reduced to the base denominator of appealing to electorates and interest groups; the defeat of the KMT in the 2000 presidential election by the independence–minded Democratic Progressive Party (DPP) has played into the hands of those in Taiwan who take seriously the external threat from the Chinese mainland. In other words, democratisation may not be the panacea it is often portrayed, and the Taiwan example illustrates that democratisation adds its own challenges to the security agenda. We also see on Taiwan how the identity issue has encroached upon security. While both sides of the Taiwan Strait struggle over their own interpretation of 'Chinese', for forty years an amalgamation of minority identities were suppressed on Taiwan by the dominating 'mainlander' mentality. Together with the threat from Communist China, this justified both the absence of democracy in Taiwan and the importance of martial law.

All of these issues are addressed in the following pages, although the discussion is concerned above all with the media. Statistics reveal that Taiwan is a media–dominated society: In mid–1999, Taiwan had on average 3.61 radio receivers and 1.37 television sets per household (though many families had a significantly higher number than the average); terrestrial telecasting reached 99.47 percent of all households and cable penetration was as high as 80 percent; in 2000, there were 433 newspapers, 6,451 magazines and 142 radio stations.[2] Clearly Taiwan today is a media–friendly society that deserves serious attention.

The central hypothesis that drives this study is that the media provide a useful measure of either the presence of democracy or the lack of it. We then proceed to discuss that the media have therefore played a leading role in the *conception* of security in Taiwan, and in the very *practice* of making Taiwan secure. The media have thus been a channel used by the political authorities to transmit their idea of how Taiwan – or more accurately, the Republic of China – might be made more secure from interference by the Chinese communists in Beijing. At the same time the media have been fundamental to the consolidation and exercise of power by a political party that has struggled to enjoy legitimacy in Taiwan. The media have been at the centre of some of the most vicious contests between the government and the opposition, outlawed until 1987; they have served as surrogate political organisations, and have been made the scapegoat by the government for crises that threatened to undermine their political authority. In short we contest that it is *impossible* to discuss the process of democratisation in Taiwan without considering the role of the media, and without introducing to the argument fundamental questions of security. As Norberto Bobbio (1987) suggests, even a 'minimal definition' of democracy requires the full realisation of what he terms 'the so–called basic rights: freedom of opinion, of expression, of speech, of assembly, of association, etc.' Robert Dahl's (1991) 'polyarchies' similarly feature protecting basic freedoms of expression and access to forms of communication that are not controlled by the state.

We should not confine the discussion to the internal effects of the media on democratisation and security. The 'Third Wave' of democratisation was particularly impressive because of the remarkable contagion effects of international communications flows. The reception of media products in foreign territories allows people in similar circumstances to see the world beyond their borders, and who might then adopt or adapt the model of transition they see abroad. So, 'Global communications networks not only demonstrate to people in one country that autocrats can be successfully removed in another; they often show how it can be done!' Most of the democratisation that enveloped Eastern Europe at the end of the 1980s can be explained partly by the contagion effects of news broadcast around the region by the mass media there (Taylor, 1997; Karl & Schmitter, 1994). Likewise Iran in the 1990s experienced the organisation of clandestine media flows. High–school graduates began to make pirate copies of films and television programmes received in Iran from neighbouring countries and hired then out to friends and neighbours[3] (much as the 1979 revolution there was incited by illegal recordings of speeches by Ayatollah Khomeini. See Mohammadi, 1997). This can help explain why many states have tried to limit the reception of foreign media products by their own people, a paranoia captured in the continuing debate about the relevance of 'cultural imperialism', the attempt to homogenise culture into a standard defined by a dominant power (usually the United States). Cultural Imperialists see existing media relations as encouraging further division between rich and poor, the northern and southern hemispheres, based on the imbalance in access to media technology and lack of control over the media agenda. In short, world patterns of communication flows mirror the system of domination in the economic and political orders. Societies feel that their fragile national identities are threatened by the inappropriate content of imported media. In India, many foreign (American) soap operas are collectively referred to as 'cultural invaders'. One former Prime Minister of India painted an apocalyptic vision: 'What we have preserved over the past 5,000 years could be eliminated by the foreign media' ('Blushing India Seizes Cosmo', *Sunday Times*, 30 March 1997). The *Tehran Times* said that Iranians were 'the silent victims of this invasion'.

Foreign programmes, it noted in similar militaristic terms, were a 'threat to the integrity and solidity of families and societies. ... We are facing an enemy and not a rival. We should not let them win' ('Iran Bans Corrupting Satellite Television', *Guardian*, 2 January 1995) Countries as different from each other as China and France have tried to circumvent cultural imperialism by imposing yet another monopoly on information. They may ban satellite dishes, or set a quota for the amount of foreign films and television programmes that can be imported. The rise of a more protectionist global media environment is an understandable response to perceived threats to the security of national identity. However, in an increasingly interdependent world with information circumnavigating the globe faster than at any time in the past – especially with the growing use of the internet – it is questionable just how much longer such states can hold out against the communications revolution. We even have evidence that the removal of protectionist regulations can *stimulate* quality competition to cultural imports: The removal of quotas on American films in Korea in 1999 has rejuvenated the Korean film industry (*Far Eastern Economic Review*, 20 July 2000).

We are also interested in the implications of democratisation for the institutions of the mass media in Taiwan. We contest that these are matters of critical importance and urgency for understanding the continuity and changes in modern political systems. We have been faced by a series of conceptual challenges in our observations of the media in Taiwan. As is illustrated in this introduction finding satisfactory definitions for 'democracy' and 'critical security' has been problematic, though we take comfort from the fact that we do not face such difficulties alone. Other problems are more obstinate: the media do not stand separately from society, they are embedded in it. We therefore find it almost impossible to determine the effects of the media on society, and whether any hypothetical consequences could more accurately be attributed to the behaviour of other actors within the social system. One way to remedy this is to constantly remind ourselves that the media *mediate*. They rarely act as independent social actors, but are involved in a relationship with them – media corporations, political interests, the electorate, the citizenship. These relationships structure this book. Important here is the understanding that the *messages* of media products are arguably less important to our understanding of their significance in democracy than their *effects* on the political process and agenda. The historic Presidential election of 18 March 2000 that overturned fifty years of rule by the Nationalist KMT and elected as President a man that the party had previously jailed for his political convictions, has sent shock–waves through Taiwan that have reverberated around the region and have been felt in the US. While the people of Taiwan are to be congratulated on their courage in electing a DPP–supported President – one might wish to paraphrase Mao Zedong (as in fact Chen Shui–bian did in his inauguration speech) and claim that the Taiwanese people have at last 'stood up' – it is without doubt that Taiwan is now embarking on an uncertain path. Chen has pledged to 'maintain the sovereignty, dignity and security' of Taiwan, and pledged what has become known as the 'five no's. In short, Chen has pledged that 'as long as the CCP [Chinese Communist Party] regime has no intention to use military force against Taiwan,' he will not change the country's name, declare independence, codify Lee's 'state–to–state' relations into the constitution, promote a referendum to decide Taiwan's future, and will not abolish the National Unification Guidelines established by his predecessors in the Presidential Office (*Taipei Times*, 6 June 2000). One commentator criticised these declarations as weakening Taiwan while China prepares for war (Li Thian–hok, *Taipei Times*, 6 June 2000).

It remains too early to speculate how his Presidency and the new security agenda that his election victory promises will affect the media, though in the Conclusions we do provide an as up–to–date analysis as possible of the post–election scenario. Chen's problems are compounded by the fact that cross–Strait relations have become re–militarised. After the increase in interaction between Taipei and Beijing that began in the 1980s, the relationship has moved steadily back towards confrontation, due mainly to China's military modernisation programme and Taiwan's efforts to improve its defence capabilities. At the same time, we cannot dismiss the time–factor. It is possible that both will recognise that time to find a favourable solution to their problems is running out. China feels that Taiwan is moving towards independence, a conviction no doubt fuelled by Chen Shui–bian's election victory, and that only military pressure will prevent a formal declaration.[4] In turn, Taiwan identifies China's military build–up as a threat to security making Taipei less agreeable to compromise. So although Taiwan's security policy has evolved from 'an aggressive "recovery of the mainland" strategy to "Taiwan as a separate and equal political entity" defence posture', the China threat is still real (Chiou in Booth & Trood, 1999). Taiwan must therefore maintain a military strength that is able to deter China from attacking, and repel any aggression that might take place. The difficulties were outlined by the Ministry of Defense in 1996: Taiwan does not seek military confrontation with China, with whom Taipei hopes to develop peaceful relations. However, until those hopes are realised Taiwan's military must remain on high alert (*China Times*, 7 July 1996; 11 July 1996).

Taiwan's predicament, described at the start of this chapter and spanning just two weeks in 1999, illustrate the difficulty of trying to define security. Taiwan faces challenges that grabbed the attention of realist scholars during the Cold War and packaged security in easily digestible terms, the kind of theorising that warrants Ken Booth's description of 'fast food realism' (Krause & Williams, 1997). This embraced the centrality of the state as the principal actor in international relations, the perpetual presence of external threats to state sovereignty, and the need to militarise to meet such threats. The presence of the state is a lesser evil; threats *from* the state are less pressing than those that would arise in its absence. In one sense this is a type of security dilemma that identifies a trade–off between security and democracy. This is an *objective* interpretation of security. Taiwan has confronted a series of actual threats from China: the offshore islands of Kinmen and Matsu were periodically shelled from 1955 to 1979, sometimes as in 1958 bringing the US and USSR close to the brink of war; Chinese missile tests, conducted close to Taiwan's coast, 'coincided' with President Lee's controversial visit to the US in 1995, and again with Taiwan's first open and direct Presidential election in 1996. As demonstrated by the 50th anniversary of the PRC communist rhetoric that promises the possibility of a Chinese military invasion of the island continues.

However, we must be mindful that there are examples that seem to contradict the idea of a corollary between the level of democracy and external security. Russell Trood and Ken Booth (1999) remind us that two of the most democratic states in the Asia–Pacific region – Australia and New Zealand – have been among the most active military powers. At the same time, those states that have been the least active in the international arena have also been the most repressive at home – Burma, Indonesia and Thailand, for example. We also need to be aware that the realist scenario can over simplify the multi–ethnic character of 'nation–states' in the region, and that it is difficult to discover the 'authentic voice of a particular polity':

> In Asia ... the typical state is a multi–nation construct, with one dominant (imperial) nation. ... The propagandistic language of the 'nation–state' attempts to hide multi–ethnic realities. 'Blackboxing' political units such as states serves not only the interests of neorealist oversimplifying, but also the political interests of the dominant ethnic groups or traditional political elites (Trood & Booth, 1999).

This is clearly the case in Taiwan where, until the 1990s, a dominant minority exercised power as the state, and imposed its political and social values upon a majority indigenous nation. This conflict of identity will play itself out many times in the following discussion.

This leads us to a second approach to security that calls for a *subjective* interpretation. This suggests that the threats from an external power are used more to secure *internal* benefits than *external* security. This corresponds to the broad definition of critical security which postulates that the origin of the greatest threat to a *nation's* security is often the *state* itself: 'The state is a major source of both threats to and security for individuals. Individuals provide much of the reason for, and some of the limits to, the security–seeking activities of the state' (Buzan, 1991). The central premise of our analysis of Taiwan is that it is essential to combine both approaches; that a real or perceived threat can justify the way a government responds to internal challenges to its power:

> The appeal to national security as a justification for actions and policies which would otherwise have to be explained is a political tool of immense convenience for a large variety of sectional interests in all types of state. Because of the leverage over domestic affairs which can be obtained by invoking it, an undefined notion of national security offers scope for power–maximizing strategies to political and military élites. ... the natural ambiguity of foreign threats during peacetime makes it easy to disguise more sinister intentions in the cloak of national security (Buzan, 1991; also see Lipschultz, 1995).

We do not wish to enter into the debate typified by that between Ken Booth and Mohammed Ayoob on the relationship between the state and security (Krause & Williams, 1997). We contest that it is possible to analyse the subject using the best from both worlds. Ayoob contributes the understanding of security and state–building, especially in the Third World. His analysis is useful as it draws our attention to the problems faced by the KMT in Taiwan. While not intended to excuse the sometimes harsh treatment meted out to the opposition, we nevertheless need to be aware of how the need for objective security impinged upon domestic politics:

> The state remains the principal vehicle and guardian of the most powerful mobilizing ideas and destructive capabilities in political life: patriotism and nationalism (Falk, 1995).

States after all do provide an effective protection against external intervention.[5]

At the same time, the non–statist approach is valuable as it sharpens our awareness of how states are no longer *the* principal political actor. As the world opens up to a more fluid understanding of identity, we discover that there are shifting forms of association that make competing claims on our loyalty and affection (Falk, 1995). Moreover, a primarily state–centric approach to international relations and security has difficulty in coming to terms with the non–local problems of the post Cold War agenda: human rights, famine, refugees, terrorism, disease and the environment all pose challenges to international security that can not be managed by states in isolation from each other. We can also acquire a greater insight into this convergence of national identities by raising an interesting question – one that we do not intend to answer, merely to pose as an example of the way it is impossible to approach the subject from one exclusive model – about the security of Taiwan: did the sudden influx of 'mainlanders' (the transplant of the Republic of China) between 1947 and 1949 actually expand the threats to Taiwan by dragging the island and its people into the Chinese civil war? This civil character of the war between the 'two Chinas' in fact blurs the distinction between the traditional agendas. The confusion of national and international, citizens and foreigners, add to the difficulty of identifying the referent in any discussion of Taiwan's security. The security problems that Taiwan faces have been summarised by C.L. Chiou (in Booth & Trood, 1999) in the following way. Taiwan's 'strategic culture'[6] displays all the characteristics of:

> a deep traditional sense of insecurity; great fear of Chinese communist aggression and acceptance of the fact that Taiwan cannot win a military confrontation with China; a desperate need to have sufficient force to defend Taiwan against the China threat ... and to maintain semi–official alliance relations with the US; an anti–militarist attitude, disliking and mistrusting the military and use of force to settle disputes; ... a desperate need and struggle to be an active and respected member of the international community; ... an evolving attitude and belief that economic power, ties and interdependence, not military power and confrontation, should be the foundation of national security ... and Lee Teng–hui's stance ... not to succumb to the 'China threat', to maintain a separate and independent Taiwanese identity and to attain high international visibility and acceptance.

On paper Taiwan's transition to democracy is impressive, as the following 'checklist' provided by the *Free China Review* in (February) 1996 makes clear:

[L]egislative representatives elected through free and fair elections and endowed with real power; equal campaigning opportunities and fair election laws, polling, and tabulation of ballots; people organized in three major political parties and many smaller ones; and a significant opposition vote and realistic possibility for the opposition not only to increase their support, but also to gain power through elections. Moreover, everyone is represented; no cultural, ethnic, religious, or other minority groups are denied reasonable self–determination. ...

This discussion will contest several of the above assertions with reference to the media. For example, we can challenge the rather naïve notion that parties and candidates in elections enjoy equal campaigning rights and opportunities; the advantages of incumbency and the tendency of the media to still focus on a small selection of favourable politicians remains a problem in a 'democratic' system. We might also question the equal representation of ethnic groups by examining the cultural politics of the KMT government as reflected through the media. The list of achievements continues:

Taiwan also has a full slate of civil liberties: ... freedom of assembly and demonstration; freedom to form and operate political parties, civic associations, trade unions, and other professional and private organizations. Moreover, citizens are equal before the law, have access to an independent judiciary, and are protected from arbitrary imprisonment. And freedom of religious expression, freedom of movement, choice of residence, property rights, and choice of marriage and size of family are all taken for granted.

More provocative is the inclusion in this list of 'full ... civil liberties' of the declaration that Taiwan has 'a free and independent media; an environment of free and open discussion, public and private ...' This book will examine how the political transition of the Republic of China has not been a panacea for the problems that surfaced in an earlier age. Nor will it agree that the media now occupy an ideal location within society. Rather, the democratisation has exposed other problems, such as the challenges to programming quality by market forces, and the continued intimidation of journalists by government agencies. The media are unable to enjoy absolute freedom even though they may be outside the state structurally; they are restricted by market competition.

A libertarian model of the press also requires the introduction of the idea of social responsibility. This suggests that while the media accept they are subject to the 'hidden hand' of the market, they must also recognise and fulfil their responsibilities to society. This assumes that the media organisations are able to identify their responsibilities and are animated by a paternal sense of their power. Inevitably there are serious problems with this model, not least because it depends far too much on the social conscience of owners who are driven by other motives – namely profit – more than duty (Siebert, Peterson & Schramm, 1956). This prompts the question, how should a media organisation reconcile the need for freedom from political interference with the need for a state mechanism that regulates the more ugly features of market capitalism? Is a regulatory framework inevitably anti–libertarian (Keane, 1991; Negrine, 1994)? Such line of inquiry then leads to a consideration of '[H]ow much freedom should broadcasters have, given that they have almost monopolistic control over the means of mass communication?' (Negrine, 1994). Such issues determine the way the media have been used for, and have been viewed as, a challenge to national security in many countries, including Taiwan.

The premise of this discussion is that the democratisation of the *political system* is now complete. Since the launch of reform in 1986, few observers were satisfied with its progress until Taiwan experienced a change of government. This seemed peculiar as it appeared to contradict the very essence of Schumpeterian procedural democracy – the right of the people to choose their government. While accepting that problems remain in political systems dominated by single parties, especially corruption and state patronage (Gilomee & Simkins, 1999; Robinson & White, 1998), is there reason to be despondent if a party is repeatedly voted into power by a well–informed citizenry in free and open elections? After all, a 'preoccupation with free and fair elections as the litmus test of democratic legitimacy obscures the restricted nature of new democracies, many of which have weak institutional foundations and a substantial degree of 'illiberalism'' (Robinson & White, 1998). With the victory of the DPP's Chen Shui-bian in the 2000 Presidential election, pushing the KMT into an embarrassing third-place (behind the 'maverick' independent James Soong), it is difficult to sustain the argument that political democratisation has yet to run its course. However, this book will also suggest that problems linger, many of which impinge upon the media – state surveillance and a persistent climate of fear that prevents journalists from performing their duties in a free and open manner. Together with the continuing influence of the PRC over Taiwan's political, and therefore media, agenda (infringing sovereignty) we are more hesitant than many to pronounce Taiwan a *full* democracy. We agree with Gilomee and Simkins (1999) that the present political system on Taiwan (along with South Africa, Mexico and Malaysia) represents 'unfinished history'.

Nevertheless Taiwan has made remarkable progress since the process of political reform began in 1986. Taiwan enjoys a level of democracy that satisfies the hunger for a 'procedural minimum' (Gilomee & Simkins, 1999). Not surprisingly, Taiwan's democratisation has been the subject of renewed interest, as suggested by the sudden proliferation of English–language studies on the political transformation there.[7] Most understandably focus on the transformation of state institutions, the development of pluralism, and the now institutionalised electoral culture. They discuss at length the persistence of factional politics, the problem of political corruption and vote buying. Post–earthquake Taiwan has also seen the sudden and welcome growth of an active civil society that mobilised to help their fellow countrymen. The '921 Earthquake Disaster Victim Coalition' has been the most vocal of the hastily convened civil organisations to campaign on behalf of the earthquake's victims (*Taipei Times*, 10 October 1999). This group is typical of a new breed of non–partisan issue–based groups that are prepared to defy the authorities to demonstrate on behalf of their convictions. In December 1997, significant amendments to the Criminal Procedure Code provide a further guarantee for civil rights through the due process of criminal justice, while the so–called 'Miranda Warning' insists that police officers must give fair notice to suspects before interrogating them – a suspect must be 'read his rights' for his answers to be admissible in a court of law.

Why the majority of these studies of Taiwan's democratisation fail to devote sufficient attention to the role of the mass media is less understandable.[8] The mass media – print, TV, radio, and now even the Internet – have been at the core of Taiwan's political landscape since the 1940s. They have acted as transmission belts for the state and have provided the focus of organised opposition to it. Simply put, the media are a vital conduit of relations between state and society. As in many other political systems that have faced similar challenges of state–building, the government decided to respond to media–led provocation by hounding journalists and silencing them. Journalists have been exiled, imprisoned, or worse. At the same time, we should not lose sight of the fact that the media have been a powerful force for the weakening of authoritarian rule, have helped to structure participation and competition within the political arena, and have thus made a positive contribution to the consolidation of democratic procedure (Laufer & Paradeise, 1989). The media have provided a voice for those who are alienated from the political process, and arouse a better informed citizenry. The media help to critically assess state action and provide essential information that may constrain the centralisation of power. It can be argued convincingly that those features of Taiwan's transition that have contributed to its unique character and success – a smooth and gradual liberalisation characterised by rapid economic growth with, by 1980, the most equitable pattern of income distribution among all developing countries[9], a remarkable degree of inclusiveness, and an almost complete absence of violent confrontation between the government and the opposition[10] – were served by a highly developed mass–media and one of the most literate societies in Asia.[11] These factors seem to validate Howard Wiarda's 1985 expectations that as 'countries achieved greater literacy, were more strongly mobilized, and acquired more radio and television sets, they would also tend to become more politically developed – i.e., liberal and democratic'. In short, Taiwan's recent experiences of regime transition suggest the existence of a strong correlation between the promotion of free and diverse media and the levels of democratic change.[12]

Today the government of the ROC itself accepts that free and diversified media are essential components of democratic change. Former director–general of the GIO, Jason C. Hu, has described the 'unfettered flow of information' as a 'prerequisite for democratic development':

> Deregulating the news media allows media professionals to handle information according to the best of their ability and free judgement. It is extremely important for the media to make information available, serve as a government watchdog, make social assessments, and resolve conflicts. Therefore, the government as well as the public should respect and safeguard the independence of the media in their role as an impartial fourth estate that checks and balances the executive, legislative and judicial branches of the government (Hu, 1994).

There remain, however, obstacles to the fulfilment of this vision. The most important is the way journalists often feel that they need to conduct their business behind close doors because of the threat of legal retribution. Packages of documents are discreetly passed from anonymous sources, telephones are tapped, offices are searched, and sometimes journalists and their sources stand in court accused of treason. Most likely the information that is at the centre of such activity does not concern secret nuclear weapons programmes or covert operations against China. It does not even present a threat of internal subversion that would undermine the very fabric of life in Taiwan. Usually the information concerns government property dealings or maybe political relations with the criminal underworld. Laws that clarify what is classified and what may be placed in the public domain are vague and open to interpretation. Journalists must rely for information either on the GIO, a source of invariably 'good' news about Taiwan, or on anonymous sources, cultivated through personal contact. Being such a source carries dangers, as Lo Chih–hau, secretary to a former transport minister, discovered as late as August 1999. Lo was accused of having sold information to journalists about delicate aviation negotiations between Taiwan and Cambodia, Thailand and Hong Kong – 'information that would prompt China to block progress of the talks and thus harm the island's interests' (*Taipei Times*, 7 October 1999). He also allegedly sold the cockpit recordings from a China Airlines plane that crashed in Taipei in 1998 killing 202 people. The government authorised the search of a weekly magazine and the homes of two newspaper reporters whose telephones were bugged for more than two years. Lo was subsequently caught and charged with the 'theft of private property.'[13] The Taipei Press Guild has resisted such clandestine government interference, claiming it is an 'infringement of press freedom' (*China News*, 3 August 1999). The full text of its statement is instructive for it reveals how the media view their own responsibilities and relationship with government in a democratic age. It also draws the battle–lines between the media and government:

> We firmly believe that the people should have the right to know, and that without this right, the people cannot elect an incorruptible and efficient government;
> The government is authorised to by the people to serve the people, but without press freedom and control through public opinion, this authorisation is vulnerable;
> The government that interferes in news coverage and freedom of speech always thinks it is justified, and autocratic and dictatorial governments often use the pretext of "national security" as an excuse for such interference;
> The government that really believes in democracy and freedom should implement regulations to prevent the leakage of information that could do harm to the nation and the people, instead of constituting laws to restrict journalistic freedom. ...
> We hope that the nation as a whole will understand that reporters have no more privilege than does the public, but that if the freedom of covering, reporting and commenting on current events is infringed by the government in any way, we will lose the democracy that we presently enjoy (*China News*, 3 August 1999).[14]

Most worrying is the possibility that the trial will encourage media to be more concerned with self–censorship for fear of becoming targets of criminal investigation. There is a chance that fewer reporters will have the courage to scrutinise the activities of government officials and will thus be denied the opportunity to create a genuine 'fourth estate'. At the same time that such implications of the Lo case were reverberating through Taiwan (election candidates, including Chen Shui–bian and James Soong have repeatedly voiced their concern that they are the victims of illegal wire–tapping[15]), the first allegations of bugging and screening the e–mail communications of specific individuals at the Ministry of Justice were reported (*Taipei Times*, 1 September 1999).

The tacit acceptance of bugging communications as a justified state–directed activity is perhaps as worrying as the actual practice itself. The Legislative Yuan is called upon to discuss the annual budget for telephone surveillance operations, while Chunghwa Telecom, a state–run company employs 200 people in its 'wiretapping unit'. Moreover, The *Taipei Times* (1 November 1999) reported that in December 1999 the police were opening a telephone wire–tapping centre for northern Taiwan after years of argument with the Investigation Bureau over who should have responsibility for such activity. Finally the two had managed to work out a compromise and now enjoy a clearly–defined division of labour![16] It has even been revealed that 'over 10,000 home's phones in greater Taipei are regularly monitored' (*Taipei Times*, 6 November 1999).

Hence the excitement among journalists over the so–called 'sunshine laws' at the end of 1999. Officially known as the Freedom of Information Act, the National Secrets Act, and the Archives Act, these would provide journalists a clear indication of which information is public property, and which is not. Administrators would no longer have the power to arbitrarily determine which documents are classified; that task will fall to a neutral legal department. The Laws will also tell journalists and, more importantly for the expansion of democratic procedure and accountability in Taiwan, citizens how to access such public information. The government would no longer exercise absolute authority in preventing journalists from having access to possibly sensitive information. It is likely that the 'sunshine laws' will be delayed in the Legislature for some time to come, and then emerge with significant compromises to their strength, scale and enforcement. How would the media react to the following words penned by another director–general of the GIO, C.J. Chen, in a publication titled *Taiwan's Media in the Democratic Era*?

> In reviewing the status of Taiwan's media in the democratic era, it is important to recognise the close relationship between freedom of speech, freedom of the press, and the progress of democracy, the interplay of which is often more apparent in the Republic of China than anywhere in the rest of the world.

More useful and relevant to Taiwan's experience are Vicky Randall's observations that conclude her 1993 paper on the media in the Third World:

> Generally they [the media] have responded eagerly to the new democratic openings and opportunities, but they have been better at knocking down the old regime than in positively shaping the new. This limitation, a consequence partly of continuing government influence but above all of market forces, will assume still greater significance in the consolidation phase but need not presage the return of overtly authoritarian rule (Randall, 1993).

In the rush to praise the liberalisation of the media in Taiwan, we should not neglect the danger of the public sphere losing autonomy to commercial interests. As this volume will argue unregulated market forces can be as damaging as state interference. Normative discourse that promotes the idea of the media offering a forum for reasoned debate by an informed citizenry gives way to a consumerist society where markets and advertisers rule (Habermas, 1962). While *in theory* the market should provide pluralism and diversity in media (television) output, reality has demonstrated that market forces have forced media to converge on the middle–ground to compete for the largest audiences using standardised formats – a homogenisation of media output. In other words the market is far from being a panacea for the problems of authoritarian government. Both harm the possibility that the media might strengthen citizenship.

The Media and Critical Security

> *'The press [is] the only tocsin of a nation. [When it] is completely silenced ... all means of a general effort [are] taken away'*
> – Thomas Jefferson.

The early defenders of press freedom were all committed to the idea that state interference represented the most serious threat to democracy. Writing on the development of the press since the 'English revolution', John Keane (1991) reminds readers that 'the call for "liberty of the press" was a vital aspect of the modern democratic revolution. It prompted a search for new, more secular and democratic ways of regarding the modern state in Europe and America'. This had to be reconciled with the state's conviction that the press represented a serious threat to its security and stability. Thus the virulent debate on press freedom opened in the 17th Century, with such writers are Milton, Bentham and Tocqueville contributing to the discussion.

These writers represent the liberal tradition that advocated the media's freedom of speech and opinion, and their safety from government interference, and their ideas served as the basis for the first amendment of the American constitution ('Congress shall make no law ... abridging the freedom of speech or of the press'). By the beginning of the 20th Century the idea that the media could exercise their own power was taking hold, and the conception of the 'fourth estate', implying that the media could act as a genuine institution of political representation, was popularised. Thomas Carlyle (1907) described the press as 'a power, a branch of government, with inalienable weight in law–making' whose authority and legitimacy derived from the popular will. The liberal tradition was rooted in the advocacy of free market forces that allegedly promote media diversity and a source of resistance to arbitrary state power.

If we apply the normative evaluations of the role of the media in enhancing citizenship, we can make the following observations. To function as citizens and participate fully in the democratic process, people must be allowed full access to information and the means to evaluate it. Second, they must be allowed full access to open channels of communication that allow them to articulate their criticism of the political system, mobilise opposition to policy choices and articulate alternatives. Third, they must be able to identify with the representations of society that are communicated, and must be able to challenge and contribute to these representations. Failure to do so will only alienate them from the political system and the communications media. To facilitate these rights communication media should offer diversity in provision and the mechanisms for effective response. In turn, the consumers of the media should have equal access to their products regardless of their level of income. In denying their populations these rights, many political systems (including Taiwan in the past) have simply used the media as a source and instrument of power.

According to Denis McQuail (1987), the media are effective agencies of power because they can do one or more of the following:

- Attract and direct attention
- Persuade in matters of opinion and belief
- Influence behaviour
- Confer status and legitimacy
- Define and structure perceptions of reality.

McQuail then uses these functions to ask a series of important questions that will guide the reader to a more astute understanding of the role of the media in a given society:

- Who controls the media and in whose interest?
- Who has access to the media and on what terms?
- Whose version of the world (social reality) is presented?
- How effective are the media in achieving their social ends?
- What variable factors limit or enlarge the power of the media in the respects mentioned?

This analysis suggests that, until 1987, Taiwan could be described as possessing an example of what McQuail refers to as a 'dominant' media landscape that engaged in a command form of communication with audiences. This embraces both mass society theory, shaped by the political theorising of C.W Mills (media controlled by monopolies with an absence of democratic regulation; the media used as channels of authority and instruction; non–dialogical; audiences demand to be led and help formulate their own ideas) and neo–Marxist theories of power (the media are mechanisms of repression due to their centralisation, bureaucratic control, and audience passivity. Enzensberger, 1970. Marxists, on the other hand, approach the media from the perspective of political–economy. The Marxist critique focuses on capitalism and market forces that prevent free information through structured ownership and the commodification of culture.) In short, the dominant model describes the media as subservient to other means of political and social control. The media are owned by a small number of powerful interests who instruct them to disseminate an 'undifferentiated' view of the world. Ownership patterns therefore impinge on the political agenda. The media are the instrument of political and economic legitimacy, and they try to preserve a common set of values, ideas and perceptions that have been defined by the government. These often provide a continuous symbolic environment that structures the framework of interpretation of audiences and their political discourse. In turn, audiences are constrained and/or conditioned to accept the messages and have little incentive or inclination to criticise. They are subject to the government's assumption that they are subordinate and dependent on the state. Audiences express little desire to seek alternative channels of information, where of course alternatives exist. Patterns of communication are unequal, one–directional and involuntary (McQuail, 1987). This 'dominant model' removes the problems associated with Marxist economic determinism – in particular too little emphasis on the state as a source of threat to media independence – from the equation. Thus the Marxist model has difficulty in understanding how the media operate in authoritarian state systems (especially those that do not subjugate market economic forces). The dominant model also has difficulty in separating the 'discourses' and 'practices' of different types of media and genre by relying on dubious quasi–scientific methodologies associated with semiology (Scannell, 1989). It is not surprising that the Marxist critique of the media is unable to shed any light on how Taiwan's media were subject to state control during the period of martial law on the island.

We in the west are familiar with patterns of media–state relations that defy the premise of the media as an independent 'fourth estate' that scrutinises the government. The British Broadcasting Corporation (BBC) is viewed with contempt by the government of the day, whatever its political hue. The controversy over the 1985 BBC documentary, *Real Lives: At the Edge of the Union*, demonstrate quite clearly how governments still interference in the media of democracies.[17] Other examples include the so–called Zircon spy affair of 1986–7, and government criticism of Kate Aidie's reporting from Libya during the American bombing of that country (Negrine, 1994). During the war against Iraq in 1991 many critics of the BBC labelled it the 'Baghdad Broadcasting Corporation' (Taylor, 1992).

The United States too has had its fair share of government interference in the media. Many conservatives still hold to the tenuous assumption that the American media 'lost' the Vietnam war which, together with Watergate and the decline of the imperial presidency, was seen to be at the core of America's descent in the 1970s (Hallin, 1986). The media were synonymous with the collapse of the American dream and the deference to authority that had been sustained by a clearly defined Cold War consensus from the end of the Second World War to the late 1960s. With the 'campus bums' that were protesting against the war in Vietnam the media were a threat to Nixon's 'silent majority' and thus the security of the nation. It is not surprising that media management of the Gulf War was designed as much to 'kick the butt' of the 'Vietnam syndrome once and for all' as to win the conflict against Saddam Hussein (Taylor, 1992).

We should be neither surprised nor shocked, therefore, when the emerging democracies are experiencing similar problems. While researching this book the press reported that similar situations to the ones described here under Taiwan's martial law were still being contested in other places. In Iran a leading pro–reform politician was indicted by a clerical court as part of a larger campaign to prevent supporters of the 'liberal' President from standing as candidates in the parliamentary elections.   The first victim was the editor of *Khordad*, a progressive newspaper that advocates reform and was closed down by a special clerical court.   The editor was accused of religious and political dissent based on articles published in the newspaper.   The closure of *Khordad* followed the banning of other pro–reform publications, *Neshat* and *Salam*, the closure of which sparked the worst wave of student protests since the 1979 revolution (*Taipei Times*, 14 October 1999).   Such pressure did not stop the reformists winning a decisive victory in the election on 18 February 2000 (*The Economist*, 26 February – 3 March 2000).

The Malaysia bureau chief of the *Far Eastern Economic Review*, Canadian citizen Murray Hiebert, was released from a jail in Malaysia in October 1999 having spent two years behind bars.   He was found guilty of contempt following an article published in the *Review* that spotlighted a trend of defamation suits in Malaysia.   He 'now feels a duty to champion the cause of press freedom for colleagues worldwide' (*Taipei Times*, 14 October 2000).   Just a month later Malaysia's political opposition complained that they were denied access to the mainstream mass media, dominated by the ruling party, even though the country was going to the polls in a general election.   The opposition said the press refused to run their campaign advertisements, while newspapers, television and radio were blanketed by stories, advertisements and editorials endorsing the Prime Minister's Barisan Nasional (BN) coalition.   This is hardly surprising when one considers that mainstream newspapers and the state–run and private television stations   are either owned by the government or controlled by interests linked to the ruling coalition.   Publishing laws that require newspaper owners to apply for annual licenses, allow the government to shut down offending newspapers or revoke their licenses.   Underground newspapers, especially *Harakah*, have gained in popularity since 1998 with a circulation to rival the mainstream press (*Taipei Times* 24 November 1999).[18]

In Taiwan, journalists from the press and the broadcast media still find themselves subject to myriad legal and extra–legal restrictions, ranging from state and political ownership/influence in the media, to the absence of a well–defined Freedom of Information Act, to regular surveillance and bugging.   Journalists covering election campaigns and politics know that their telephones are bugged and their sources monitored.[19]

These examples all suggest the continuing relevance of the state. Even if we disaggregate its institutions to form a more bureaucratic oriented study, we cannot escape the centrality of the state.   Rather we must ensure that the focus centres more on the interaction of the state with society.   Only then will we be able to understand how the media have contributed to a healthier understanding of security, rather than being merely the public outlet for bureaucratic struggles. This study appreciates the role of elite interaction in the collapse of authoritarianism in Taiwan: it is pointless to discuss democratisation there without mentioning the vision and commitment of Chiang Ching–kuo and Lee Teng–hui. We contest, however, that civil society and the various institutions around it, including the previously illegal opposition movements, were more than secondary actors in the process. We concur with Gill (2000) that civil society must be located much more prominently in the transitology literature and, as in Taiwan, its activity is more than just 'background noise' (Gill, 2000). The media, often at great cost, gave voice and expression to this process and helped ensure that the transition would have a unique social as well as political dynamic.

We end this introduction with the words of Wasko and Mosco (1992) who have provided a brief yet satisfactory definition of political communications in a democratising political and social system. They drive this discussion towards any normative implications that readers might expect. As our argument unfolds, it will become clear how this normative framework has structured discourse about the relationship between politics and the media in Taiwan:

> Thus the concept of democratic communications is two–fold ...:
> 1. *democratization* of media and information or technologies, or participatory and alternative media forms and democratic uses of information technologies; and
> 2. *democratization through* media and information technologies, or media strategies of various social movements and groups devoted to progressive issues and social change.

Notes

1. 'To cite one case, a multi–billion dollar bidding project used to have to pass stages of assessments under relevant bidding regulations. But the emergency order makes it convenient for corrupt officials to skip the assessments and make decisions favourable to particular bidders' (*Taipei Times*, 15 October 1999).
2. http://www.gio.gov.tw/info/book2000/ch16_2.htm.
3. The government unleashed the fundamental Bassijis, originally organised to fight the war against Iraq, to now wage a new campaign against western spiritual pollution. They have the authority to arrest anyone caught with video or audio cassettes with western contents. See Mohammadi (1997).
4. In a pessimistic interview with the *Far Eastern Economic Review* (8 June 2000), Singapore's Senior Minister Lee Kuan Yew talked of the inevitability of reunification with China or war across the Taiwan Strait. Lee believed that Chen

had inherited a worrying trend of indigenisation from Lee Teng–hui. Indigenisation, he said, would only make reunification harder for the people of Taiwan.

5.   The extent of the state's obsession with national security extended into many areas: since 1949, the Central Weather Bureau has been responsible for all weather monitoring, and is the only organisation able to announce weather forecasts. Meteorological information is still deemed 'confidential' for purposes of national security. *Taipei Times*, 31 October 1999.

6.   'The concept of strategic culture refers to the nation's traditions, values, attitudes, patterns of behaviour, habits, symbols, achievements and particular ways of adapting to the environment and solving problems with respect to the threat and use of force' (Macmillan & Booth in Booth & Trood, 1999).

7.   In his study of *The Taiwan Political Miracle* (1997), John F. Copper suggests reasons why Taiwan has tended to be neglected by western scholars.

8.   Steven Harrell and Huang Chun–chieh (1994) have edited an excellent study of Taiwan's culture, though it only offers a brief discussion of the media. For full discussions, see Berman (1992) and Rawnsley & Rawnsley (1998). Reference is also made in Yun–Han Chu's chapter on Taiwan in Giliomee & Simkins, 1999).

9.   'The difference in income between the top and the lowest quintile in Taiwan shrank from 20 times in 1953 to 4.5 in 1980. This ... was accomplished by ... an extensive land reform ... an export–oriemted industralization strategy ... a centralized primary education system ... a conservative credit and fiscal policy ... and a large state–owned sector' (Giliomee & Simkins). Full details can be found in J. Fei, G. Ranis and S. Kuo, *Growth with Equality* (Oxford University Press, 1979).

10.   'In fact while the transition in Taiwan has been long in coming, it has nevertheless been one of the smoothest transitions among newly democratised countries' (Hood, 1997). This stands in marked contrast to the record of success of those states that have experienced abrupt change – see Huntington (1991). However, Taiwan *is* familiar with violent confrontation, and all the best political histories – including our own! – will discuss the 1947 February 28th Incident, the Chungli riots of 1977, and the Kaohsiung Incident of 1979.

11.   In 1995, the national literacy rate was 94 percent. (*Republic of China Yearbook, 1997*).

12.   An important caveat: 'A public ... exists as discursive interactional processes; atomized individuals, consuming media in their homes, do not comprise a public, nor do they tend to contribute much to the democratization of civil society. ... [F]rom the standpoints of democracy, it is imperative not to lose sight of the classic idea that democracy resides, ultimately, with citizens who engage in talk with each other'. Democracy is based on 'people interacting in their roles as citizens' (Dahlgren, 1995). Dahlgren also makes the following perceptive point that should warn media scholars against adopting simple methodologies and interpretations, especially survey analysis: 'To burlesque the point somewhat: atomized TV news viewers responding to questionnaires is not a portrait of a viable democracy.'

13.   On 22 December 1999, Loh was found guilty of having leaked information about international air negotiations, and information that concerned a bidding project for cargo terminals at Chiang Kai–shek Airport. He was sentenced to two years in jail. Other charges, including allegations of providing the media with black–box transcripts from the China Airlines crash of 1998 were dismissed. *Taipei Times*, 23 December 1999.

14.	The adversarial relationship between the media and the government was reinforced during the trial: The Taipei district prosecutor, Lee Liang–chung, said: 'It is the nature of the media to pursue information, whatever secrets there may be. But it is the job of civil servants to restrain themselves and protect national interest above anything' (*Taipei Times*, 7 October 1999).

15.	As director–general of the Government Information Office (1979–1984), Soong ordered the closure of more than forty publications. He also supported wiretaps and mailchecks. On the campaign trail in 1999, Soong justified his actions during martial law: 'As a government official, I just followed the rules' (*China News*, 8 August 1999).

16.	'The Taipei centre will monitor fixed–line calls, and will work in tandem with the already–established cellular–phone surveillance centre set up under the National Police Administration. Police will be able to monitor all fixed–line phone calls on service providers other than Chunghwa Telecom, which will remain under the jurisdiction of the Investigation Bureau' (*Taipei Times*, 1 November 1999).

17.	The BBC documentary interviewed individuals from both extremes in Northern Ireland, Republican and Loyalist terrorists. The government intervened to prevent transmission (Prime Minister Thatcher did not want to give terrorists the 'oxygen of publicity'), and the Board of Governors concurred, provoking a strike among BBC employees. See Negrine (1994).

18.	Further examples are available from the publications of Article 19: The International Centre Against Censorship.

19.	For obvious reasons, the sources of this information have requested anonymity. The authors respect their wishes.

1   Television and Power

'Among all the means of mass communications, television is the most effective. Thus the production of television programmes must not be profit–oriented. Only when television carries out the spirits of the Three Principles of the People[1] *can it be said that our television industry fulfils its social responsibilities as a medium of mass communications'.*
– President Chiang Ching–kuo (Wang, 1993).

Introduction

At the height of its power on Taiwan, the ruling Kuomintang (KMT) sought to create a television system that would be an effective instrument of political control and social construction:

> National interest and public welfare are the overriding objectives of the television enterprise. Being a mass medium is basically different from other profit–making enterprises. Cultural heritage and ethical traditions constitute the spiritual cornerstone of the nation (Lee, 1979).

The creation and development of Taiwan's television industry reveals how, for over thirty years, political and security concerns intruded in the cultural life of the island and penetrated its media. The government shared the communist conviction that broadcasting is a source of political power, and thus in the wrong hands can be a powerful force for weakening authoritarian rule and advancing democratisation. The argument for maintaining a firm grip on the media in Taiwan was therefore obvious.

For governments television is a more obliging medium than the press. The latter have throughout their global history been an actual or potential adversary to established power structures. Press history is resplendent with images – especially self–constructed images – of journalists and editors battling against political forces that would silence their voices. The press are the champions of democracy, human rights, the people, and above all, freedom of speech (Chalaby, 1998; Thompson, 1995). During martial law the 'mainstream press' in Taiwan were prevented from executing these self–proclaimed responsibilities due to party–state[2] ownership and/or influence, and a complex structure of legal or fiscal restraints (thus avoiding any notion that the press could be described as having been directly intimidated). The media operated within a patron–

client relationship with the state that mixed repression and co–optation. The media that were owned outright by the party–state were naturally its mouthpiece; other media were privately owned (usually by Chinese of mainland origin) but remained dependent on the state and enjoyed relatively unlimited autonomy in areas of society that could be delineated as non–political (though the government still exercised the arbitrary power to determine the political from the non–political. See Chapter 2). As recently as 1999 GIO publications still justified such censorship in terms of national security which, they declare, 'was the government's primary concern' from the 1950s to the 1970s (Government Information Office, 1999). The underground media, the subject of the next chapter, rose to challenge this political order, though often to great cost.

For governments seeking to expand their power television is more convenient than print. Distance, and therefore distribution are of little consequence; those political systems that have used television for political ends, including Taiwan, have tended to concentrate production and organisation in the political and geographic centre (in this case Taipei), and have controlled the distribution to the periphery. This reinforces the symbolism that attaches television to the centralisation of power. More importantly the broadcast media are immediate. They can react to events and changing situations like no other media, and their resources (including signal distribution) can be redirected with little effort in an incredibly short space of time. Television is largely a passive medium that demands little intellectual energy from audiences. Television also perpetuates an unequal relationship of power between source and audience. The ramifications of this are obvious if the source happens to be a government, or government–controlled/influenced station. Television then becomes a non–dialogical and unresponsive instrument of control and instruction.

This chapter chronicles the development of Taiwan's television industry and culture from the 1950s until the late 1980s, by which time democratisation and liberalisation had made significant progress. Running parallel to this is the evolution of Taiwan's political system. We see how the media – and television in particular – were viewed as little more than instruments of political power and authority, and that the state erected an elaborate political structure to monitor and regulate media organisation and output. Ultimately the government believed that Taiwan's security from the threat posed by Chinese communists and internal subversives depended on absolute control of the media and the consolidation of a new imposed 'national' identity. This overlooked, of course, that the protection of freedom *from* can sacrifice the freedom *to*, and that the deliberate absence of democratic rights and freedoms merely encourages the very internal threats to security that the government is trying to curtail. This is the very essence of a classic security dilemma.

Taiwan's Political Structure

Taiwan's political structure has always been the centre of controversy and bewildering to outsiders. Prior to 1996 when the first Presidential election by popular vote occurred Taiwan was neither a dictatorship nor a democracy, but a strange hybrid of both, what is often referred to in the literature as 'soft' authoritarian. The Republic of China (ROC) on Taiwan had its own popularly elected parliament, the Legislative Yuan, and system of 'national' representation in the National Assembly. Yet before political reforms were introduced in the early 1980s, more than 68 per cent of legislators and members of the National Assembly represented constituencies on mainland China to which they had been elected in 1947 and 1948.[3] Until 1996 the National Assembly chose the head of state and his deputy from the ranks of the KMT, and it alone could amend the constitution. These powers were granted in the *Temporary Provisions Effective During the Communist Rebellion (Dongyuan Kanluan shiqi lingshi tiaokuan)*, a suspension of the constitution in 1948 that was far from temporary and reinforced the KMT's structure of martial law. The provisions became law on 10 May 1948, and martial law began on 19 May 1949 when the new governor of Taiwan, Chen Cheng, announced that communist troops were moving into China's Fujian province, thus threatening Taiwan. Under martial law persons could receive the death penalty if found guilty of: spreading rumours that might incite the people to challenge the government; organising a public protest that turned violent; economic sabotage; organising strikes; destroying property that belonged to public transport; damaging public utilities; carrying illegal weapons; and encouraging demonstrations in schools and universities (Chao & Myers, 1998). From 1947 to 1987 it was considered a privilege for an ordinary citizen in Taiwan to claim any right to an impartial trial, while the judicial system was based on the military–style court martial. In this way, the KMT imposed itself on an island where it did not already enjoy a strong power–base (Gold, 1986). This nullified the need for a minimal state that drew its strength from the consent of the governed (Buzan, 1991). According to the Taipei Municipal Documentation Commission, approximately 5,000–8,000 individuals were executed during the first five years of the 'White Terror' (*Taipei Times*, 7 October 1999).

The effect of the Temporary Provisions was to 'broaden presidential power, giving the president an unlimited authority unintended by the framers of the constitution' (Tien, 1989). It also meant that the members of the National Assembly could guarantee holding on to their seats until the Provisions were terminated on 1 May 1991 (Chiu, 1993). The first free elections for a full National Assembly were held on 22 December 1991, and parliamentary elections on 19 December 1992 (Robinson, 2000; Tsang, 1993; Copper, 1997; Ferdinand, 1996).

It should be noted, however, that although the KMT was an example of a hegemonic party (Sartori, 1976) it preferred to depend on informing the people, cultivating their support and persuading them of the KMT's responsibility to govern: legitimacy based on coercion was no legitimacy, as the government learned to its cost during the 28 February incident in 1948 (see below). Hence the importance of the mass media to the KMT's exercise of power.

Two interrelated factors explain why, before liberalisation, the political system was so unrepresentative of Taiwan. First, the government thought that it alone represented the true China and believed that one day it would return to control the mainland. 'We are going back to the mainland,' the *Free China Weekly* promised throughout the 1950s, an ambition that the government popularised in a slogan that gave a clear blueprint for reunification: 'one year to get ready, two years to counter–attack, three years to drive out [the communists], and five years to total victory' (*Taipei Times*, 22 January 2000). As Steven J. Hood has observed, 'Democracy was at best a long–term goal, secondarily important to recovery of the mainland and economic development' (Hood, 1997). The KMT remained committed to the goal of introducing full democracy to Taiwan but without following a timetable for its achievement. Thus Taiwan is sometimes referred to as a 'limited democracy' (Chao & Myers, 1998).

The second reason was the continuous threat of invasion by the People's Republic of China (PRC). To borrow the title of Steve Tsang's volume, the people of Taiwan have lived *In the Shadow of China* since 1949. The 'loss' of China in 1949, and Truman's 'hands-off' policy a year later,[4] suggested that the United States had abandoned Taiwan. Very few American weapons reached the island. In January 1950 Secretary of State Dean Acheson announced that the US would not provide the KMT government with military aid or advice, despite warnings that Taiwan could be expected to soon fall to the communists. In Taiwan and throughout the US, each new day brought further rumours that the communist invasion was imminent. Such fears seemed justified when communists attacked and occupied the island of Hainan in May 1950. Acheson told Ernest Bevin, the British Foreign Secretary, that Chiang Kai–shek's regime was 'washed up,' and promised that the US 'henceforth will pursue a more realistic policy respecting China' (Borg & Heinrichs, 1980). In describing these deliberations, Warren I. Cohen has written that such sentiments expressed the widespread view that the US should administer the last rites to Chiang's regime: 'On June 2 [1949], when the China Aid Act expired, the United States would cease wasting its resources. Kuomintang China was dead', while it was only a matter of time before Taiwan fell to the communists (Ibid). The Chinese Nationalists felt they had been well and truly betrayed. Such American diffidence only evaporated with the outbreak of war in Korea, propelling Taiwan to the forefront of America's Cold War strategy (Rawnsley, 2000b).[5]

The threat to Taiwan seemed undeniable when the Chinese communists periodically shelled the offshore islands of Matsu and Kinmen first in 1954, then again in 1958. Shelling continued until 1979, though by that time the shells contained nothing more lethal than printed propaganda (Rawnsley, 2000). These threats to national security certainly justified a strengthening of state power, although we now know that the intention of the shelling was merely part of Beijing's psychological warfare strategy.[6] In classic neo-realist terms the KMT identified the security of the citizens with the security of the state, 'and by definition, those who stand outside it are threats, whether actual or potential' (Tsang, 1993). This is not entirely the case, however, and by denying the creation of a democratic political system in Taiwan until 1987, the KMT admitted that it was more concerned with holding on to power than with preventing the infiltration of communism; the government confused political opposition and calls for democracy with the perceived absence of national loyalty. The truth was much more difficult to accept and package. When the United States announced in December 1978 that it planned to normalise relations with the PRC early the next year, the KMT government responded by postponing elections and placing Taiwan on high military alert. Opposition activists expressed their sympathy with the government's position, but argued exercising democracy would actually strengthen Taiwan.

> We understand the government's anguish. ... We declare that if elections are restored, it will confirm the government's opposition to a government based on lawlessness and its desire to preserve constitutional rule. We wholeheartedly confirm that the government with courage, can resist the temptation to embrace military rule while showing its determination to promote constitutional government and unify the entire nation in an environment of peace and democracy (Chou & Myers, 1998).

The government – now under the control of Kai–shek's son, Chiang Ching-kuo – chose to remain blind to such propositions, and instead remained commited to the idea that the opposition presented an internal threat that would weaken Taiwan and make the island vulnerable to Communist infiltration: 'Enemies are everywhere, planning all kinds of ways to use any opportunity to divide us. Even some of our own people who have failed to understand the problems of our country have become the tools of the enemies, and they hold opposite ideas from our government' (Chiang Ching-kuo, volume 14, 1991). Ching–kuo was adamant that martial law was essential for the promotion of democracy: ' .. in world history there has not been a single free, democratic state like the ROC that has for so long confronted an expanding communist totalitarianism. Because of this fact, the ROC relies on law and implements martial law to preserve our nation's security and to prevent the communists from exercising all sorts of subversive activities' (Chiang Ching–kuo, volume 15, 1991). Ching–kuo was as good as his word: twelve months after the American announcement that its government planned to normalise relations with the PRC, the government in Taipei crushed the opposition during an illegal rally in Kaohsiung (see Chapter 2). Meanwhile, communist intimidation continued. Communist military exercises 'coincided' with both President Lee Teng–hui's much publicised visit to the United States in 1995, and with the 1996 Presidential election. These incidents suggest that Taiwan's security is still under threat from external forces, and thus democratisation will not be complete until such influence is at least controlled, if not eradicated.

Even today, when Taiwan seems much more self–assured of its identity and place in the international system, it is still difficult to insist either that Taiwan is a 'nation-state' in its own right, or merely a province of China. This political debate has smouldered ever since the Nationalist government was defeated in the civil war by the communists and withdrew from mainland China to Taiwan in 1949. As the political system continues to evolve, and the division of powers between branches of government are reviewed, Taiwan will be forced to redefine its status in relation to China, especially under a President who represents the pro–independence Democratic Progressive Party (DPP). This in turn will have serious repercussions on the organisation of government: will Taiwan remain a province, will it become an independent state, or is it able to maintain the status quo without having to make the ominous choice of either extreme? And, more importantly, how can security in the Taiwan Strait be cemented regardless of which path is followed? These are the questions that will face Chen Shui–bian as he settles into the Presidential office in Taipei.

Some may argue that perhaps Taiwan alone does not hold the power to make the final decision. Other international actors, especially the PRC and the United States, have a significant impact on the direction that Taiwan can take. Nevertheless, before these issues can be addressed, Taiwan will have to reassess its commitment to the 'Chinese ideology' to preserve internal security during the democratisation process. The Chinese ideology allows both sides of the Taiwan Strait to project themselves as the true guardians of Chinese culture and identity. Both subscribe to the idea of *Chung Kuo*, or China as the 'Middle Kingdom', 'centre of the universe.' In the past, the KMT based its legitimacy, and therefore state power, on the Chinese ideology. Any violation in Taiwan's political or cultural life would not be tolerated (Lee, 1979). The development of Taiwan's television system, including programming, the censorship of news and political documentaries, even the policies concerning the use of minority languages, have been profoundly influenced by this faith.

Taiwan's social character has likewise been confused by the Chinese ideology. This was a consequence of the long–term political and cultural tension within the society itself, generated by the divisions between 'Taiwanese' and 'mainland Chinese'.[7]   Both were concerned with the security of their island home from the communists, but at the same time they were also anxious to prevent challenges from each other threatening their own security. Anguish bubbled over when at least 10,000 Taiwanese were massacred by mainlanders between 28 February and mid–March 1947, an episode officially christened the 'February 28th Incident'. This was a defining moment in Taiwan's history that forced society to re–evaluate and re–structure its political attitudes. 2–28, as it is now known, also had far reaching consequences for the configuration of power over and through the media. For these reasons, the incident deserves close attention.

The Media and 2–28

As part of the Japanese empire from 1895 to 1945 the Taiwanese people suffered political, economic and cultural repression. Japan's colonisation exaggerated the already huge gap between Taiwan's rich and poor, although the latter overwhelmingly outnumbered the former. Taiwan provided a source of cheap labour for Japanese industry, and Taiwanese workers received less than half the wages for Japanese workers in the same position. The Japanese government also discouraged, even prevented, the Taiwanese from studying the humanities and social sciences, especially politics, law and philosophy. Further, between 1899 and 1918 the majority of

Taiwanese were illiterate; only 15 per cent of them graduated from primary school having learnt the Japanese language. In the Taipei Empire University, there were 139 students in 1939, and 1,666 in 1945, but only 29 and 322 respectively were Taiwanese. Again the Taiwanese were encouraged to only study subjects that the Japanese considered politically 'safe', usually agriculture and medicine (*Common Wealth*, 1992).[8] Japanese authority over Taiwan was personified in the first nine governors-general up to 1919, all of whom were active military officers. Efforts to assimilate the Taiwanese into the Japanese empire accelerated, but such activity only fed the political consciousness of the people of Taiwan, many of whom now called for autonomy. Such political movements were crushed as the Japanese empire hurtled into the Second World War; the Taiwan Communist Party, founded in Shanghai in 1928, was eliminated in 1931. After the outbreak of war with China, the Japanese became more repressive, and moved towards a policy of rapid assimilation in the empire (Gold, 1986; Lai *et al.*, 1991). Naturally the Taiwanese looked towards China as their 'motherland', and anticipated that the Chinese liberation of the island would deliver local autonomy. However, the mainland Chinese resented the Taiwanese as collaborators during the 1937–1945 war with Japan (*Common Wealth*, 1992). These suspicions did not evaporate once the war ended, but instead encouraged further strains between islanders and their supposed liberators.

At the close of the Second World War, Taiwan received climbing numbers of mainland Chinese who occupied most of the top positions in the party, government, and military – some 28,000 officials arrived on Taiwan after the Second World War. The islanders were prevented from participating in government and from satisfying their longing for greater self-rule. Such colonisation, along with the bureaucracy and corruption of governor Chen Yi's administration, generated much disappointment and resentment among the islanders against the mainland immigrants. On 28 February 1947 the simmering anger of the Taiwanese finally boiled over into a near-revolution, after an isolated (some might say trivial) incident in Taipei led to violence and rioting throughout the island. Soon the rioters were demanding the introduction of meaningful political and economic reforms (Long, 1991; Lai, *et.al.*, 1991). The KMT government on the mainland feared that the incident on Taiwan was a threat to the cohesion of China and blamed communist agitators for the violence. The issue of national security – but based on a definition of nation that excluded both Chinese communists and Taiwanese – provoked the government into shipping across the Strait some 10,000 troops to subjugate the 'revolutionaries.' Their 'fortnight-long rampage of execution, rape and pillage' (Long, 1991) has entered Taiwanese history, and the consequences have been described as 'a bloodbath bloodier than the 4 June Tiananmen massacre' (Chiou, 1995). Between 10,000 and 20,000 people died, but the targets of the massacre had been carefully selected – Taiwan's social, political and intellectual elite. A whole generation of potential Taiwanese nationalist leaders was wiped out in one fell–swoop.[9]   One might even argue that the targeting of ethnic Taiwanese for execution constituted 'genocide'. The influx of 'mainlanders' meant that Taipei's population rose by almost a quarter to 494,000 from early 1948 to September 1949. The total number of troops on the island reached between 200,000 and 30,000.

Governor Chen Yi held the free media responsible for 2–28, believing that their excessive criticism of the provincial government helped to reinforce the division between mainlanders and Taiwanese (Lai *et.al.*, 1991).   In August 1946, for example, *Peace Daily* (*Ho–ping jih–pao*) commented on the 'bad caretakers,' the KMT, who 'either openly rob or secretly steal. ... National pride,' said the paper, 'has been swept away ... the Nationalists have lost the hearts of the people' (Lai *et.al.*, 1991). Liberal orthodoxy obliges the free media to hold the decision–makers to account.   Whether this implies incitement or not is another matter all together.   The media reported 2–28, but by doing so they added to the tension because they helped to spread the news (broadcasts from Taipei, for example, could be heard in Keelung and Pan-chiao).   Their role in the revolution changed once they had been seized by the insurgents who used the media as platforms for their own demands and encouraged the revolution to continue. Identity was often invoked as justification for harsh reprisals against those involved ('Wang T'ien was executed because he "had incited the people to occupy the Taiwan Broadcasting Station and had appealed to the people to take over Taiwan and expel the mainlanders"'. Lai *et.al*, 1991). The founder and president of *Jen Min Tao Pao*, Sung Fei–ju, was charged with 'attacking the government's administration and its weaknesses.' Other victims who worked for that paper were executed, one was even burned alive. The founders of *Min Pao* were executed as leaders of the rebellion and the president was arrested. The paper was closed down for indulging in 'anti–government speech' (*Taipei Times*, 7 March 2000). Managers and journalists of many other newspapers suffered similar fates. In fact an estimated 100 members of the media were killed, arrested, or forced to flee Taiwan (*Taipei Times*, 1 September 1999). Moreover, the incident provided the basis for a more acrimonious relationship between the government and media.   Accordingly, Chen Yi closed down all those newspapers that were found to represent 'different elements *outside the Kuomintang Party* ...' (emphasis added. Lai *et.al.*, 1991).[10]   Clearly, the

KMT now intended to control the media, and this involved the projection of their own interpretation of identity and the Chinese ideology. This contradicted Chen Yi's thoughts on the media that he had set down just one month previously:

> As for the media, freedom of public opinion has been given full respect to elicit a true democratic atmosphere. Taiwan's newspapers are free to publish any criticisms of the government. Criticisms with merit are accepted. Groundless charges and wild accusations which do not merit any rebuttal, will simply be disregarded. In this age of democracy, we must have the grace to tolerate opposition, especially as it is inevitable. ... There is no need to overact to reports that distorted the facts, for the truth will eventually prevail. ... Instead of being afraid, I welcome and hope to cooperate with the press. The fact that our achievements in Taiwan have effectively counteracted all the malicious reporting about us illustrates another big step forward in our democracy (quoted in Lai*et.al*, 1991).

For forty years the trauma of 2–28 haunted Taiwan's political and social life, poisoned the relationship between Taiwanese and mainlander Chinese, and explains why the islanders were so suspicious of the KMT regime. Taiwan was left a 'sorely wounded and divided society for many decades ...' (Chou & Myers, 1998). Yet the government had tried to erase the episode from the collective conscience of the nation: it was not part of Taiwan's official, that is, sanctioned history. The opposition, on the other hand, never forgot 2–28 and until the 1980s, called on the government to 'tell the people the truth about the February 28 incident and set February 28 as "Peace Day" to narrow the gap between mainlanders and Taiwanese natives'.[11] Only in early 1990 was President Lee Teng–hui convinced that the time to reopen the case had arrived, and set up a special committee to investigate the tragedy. Their report was finally published in March 1992: the government apologised, erected a memorial to the fallen, and offered compensation to the victims' families (*Central Daily News,* 23 February – 24 March 1995). But the 'special committee' did not enjoy the freedom and authorisation of an independent truth commission, and many individuals still feel that they have been denied the opportunity to learn the scope of violations committed at that time. In fact, to date no government official has faced prosecution for his role in either the 2–28 Incident nor the thirty–eight years of martial law.

The February 28th Incident provides a dramatic illustration of how such issues as national identity, cultural reconstruction, and the search for political autonomy, have affected the programmes broadcast by Taiwan's television system. Before liberalisation of the media in 1987, the stations were reluctant to pursue politics in any depth, mirroring the popular hesitation to demand any substantial political improvement.   Indeed, it could be said that democracy was sacrificed for great stability based on economic development and industrial growth, both of which were actively encouraged by the KMT government:

> Seeing their elite and its successors systematically hunted down and murdered by the mainlanders traumatized the Taiwanese to the point that the phrase, 'politics is dangerous' became a watchword etched into their collective unconscious. Political activity became associated with a violent end (Gold, 1986).

Thus a new social character gradually formed – utilitarian, intimidated, yet politically astute, and on the surface obedient to the government: 'In seeking security, state and society are sometimes in harmony with each other, sometimes opposed. Its bottom line is about survival' (Buzan, 1991). The media were used to 'depoliticize and demobilize the public sphere' (Lee, 1992). Meanwhile, thousands fled Taiwan to Hong Kong, Japan and America. Once there they continued their political struggle to overthrow the KMT regime. These were the nucleus of the opposition movement that after the lifting of martial law would eventually challenge the KMT in legalised elections and win control of the government at the dawn of the new millennium.

Taiwan's national instinct during the Cold War was for survival, especially when its interests – stability, protection from the perceived communist threat, rapid economic growth and development – coincided with the KMT's ideology.   For the ruling party, all forms of mass communications, and especially television, were obliged to fulfil specific 'social responsibilities' (Rawnsley & Rawnsley, 1998). These all serviced, and were therefore subordinate to, the over–riding priority – the eventual recovery of the Chinese mainland. From the 1950s onwards, the KMT increasingly based its political legitimacy less on force and more on Taiwan's extraordinary economic success (Przeworski, 1991).[12] Television reflected the prevalence of this social character.   First, programmes contained little discussion of politics or public affairs. If discussion did transpire, the official line would always conclude the programme. Second, television was mainly concerned with dispensing information about national policies and issuing government orders, and provided non–controversial entertainment. The more the public was entertained, the less they would think of criticising or openly opposing the government.[13] Finally, the stations would chase every opportunity to make as much money as possible, thus violating their own principle that television should not be motivated solely by the pursuit of profit. Hence Taiwan's television system became a 'typical bureaucratic–commercial complex' (Lee, 1989). This corresponds to the 'development media theory' that McQuail (1987) has tendered to challenge the contradictions associated with the need for a media that responded to social needs in a restrictive capitalist market. In short this suggests that the media should be subordinate to the needs of the developing state. Economic and political development require that the media resist or be required to exercise their almost natural adversarial and sceptical tendencies. We agree with John Keane's (1991) criticism of this model as it applies to Taiwan: 'The "development theory" made it too easy to claim that a state's interests were at stake at the first sign of legitimate criticism'.

The Development of Television in Taiwan

How did the television industry become part of the state apparatus?

Chiang Kai–shek, the party Chairman and President of the ROC, expressed his determination to develop television in Taiwan by the end of the 1950s. His original preference was for a 'public' model that would be funded completely by the government, believing that this was the only way to guarantee political control. Pressure from two sources contributed to this decision. In 1958 the PRC had already established its first television station in Beijing, and two years later Hong Kong also opened a television channel. Chiang could not tolerate the prospect that the ROC might fall behind its rivals, especially the PRC (Chang, 1995). Lacking the necessary funding for Chiang's preferred 'public' model, the government opted instead for a partly state–controlled and partly commercial system.[14]

This historical background demonstrates the way KMT leaders interpreted the idea of public service broadcasting, by which public simply meant 'firm state control.' It also reveals that the government had created a television industry only as a political expedient. This explains why, before they established national television on the island, the KMT regime did not undertake any detailed audience research or even produce a viable business plan for the project. The state knew best. Neither did it care to design a framework suitable for the long–term development of the television industry. These attitudes continued to condition the KMT government's approach to television until its liberalisation in 1987.

Taiwan Television Enterprise (TTV), Taiwan's first television company, opened transmission on 10 October 1962 after being created by the Governor of Taiwan, Chou Chih–jou, Chiang's personal appointment to head the project. The Provincial Government provided 49 per cent of its capital and its director enjoyed a close personal relationship with Chiang's family, but lacked any experience in communications or journalism. From the start TTV was little more than an instrument of the government.

Six years later in September 1968, China Television Company (CTV) was established, having followed TTV's method of raising capital and appointing personnel. 50 per cent of its stock was owned by the KMT and its first director, Li Shih–fen, had strong ties with the party. Unlike TTV, CTV did not have any foreign shareholders, thus sharpening its native identity.

Meanwhile the Minister of Defense, Chiang Ching–kuo, decided in 1968 to embrace television technology to strengthen military and social education. Chiang decided to expand the National Education Television Station that had been organised on an experimental basis since February 1962. His idea was to create a third national television company, Chinese Television System (CTS), on air in February 1969. Since the purpose of this new station was to initiate 'total cultural warfare' (Cheng *et.al.*, 1993), it seemed appropriate to appoint as its head General Wang Sheng, a pioneer of political education within the military (Marks, 1998). 49 per cent of its stock belonged to the Ministry of Education, and 51 per cent to the Ministry of National Defense. Over the years, the ownership has changed only slightly: the government, party, and related agencies or ministries, still own the lion's share of each station. Moreover, the directors share very similar career patterns to their predecessors, that is, all have extensive background in government, party, or military service (Cheng *et.al.*, 1993; *Central Daily News* 18 October 1995; 7 & 13 June 1996).[15]

Thus Taiwan's three television stations were designed to serve the KMT. This does not mean, however, that the government formally instructed the stations about how to operate or what programmes to produce. All the actors involved in the process – political and within the media – were able to arrive at a tacit agreement about the function and structure of television. These circumstances meant that none of the television networks could keep pace with the radical political and social changes that were sweeping through Taiwan in the late 1980s and 1990s. Instead they continued to present the same old conservative programmes in order to protect their own political and commercial interests, especially during elections (Kuo, 1990; Cheng *et.al.* 1993; Chang, 1995). As soon as the party–state discovered that a non–public television system could function as they wished, and make handsome profits into the bargain, Chiang Kai–shek's preference for public television lost its attraction.

Programming Policies

According to the 1982 *Broadcasting and Television Law* TTV, CTV and CTS must be supervised by the Government Information Office (GIO), a subdivision of the Executive Yuan, and thus under the jurisdiction of Taiwan's Premier. However, under martial law the GIO worked hand in hand with the Taiwan Garrison Command (TGC), the chief institution entrusted with control over the media. This was a military agency that enjoyed a 'reputation for arbitrariness and ruthlessness' (Gold, 1986). The TGC was required to ensure the restrictive provisions of martial law were obeyed, and that included suppressing the media when necessary. Hence on the surface the GIO was technically the highest institution supervising all forms of domestic publications and electronic media, but the Garrison Command remained in de facto control until the end of martial law, at which time many TGC cadres simply transferred to the GIO (Leonard, 1991). The TGC worked alongside an elaborate internal security system that included the Investigation Bureau (equivalent to the FBI in the United States); the General Political Warfare Department; the Police ('responsible for social order'); and the KMT's own 'security network and agents in government and social units'). We are told that Overseas Chinese were also subject to surveillance, with students abroad sometimes offered payment for filing reports on their classmates. Supervising the work and budget of this elaborate apparatus was the National Security Bureau, directly responsible to the President of the ROC (via the National Security Conference), and unaccountable to the Legislative Yuan, the peoples' representatives (Gold, 1986). The KMT government had designed a complex and thorough state security structure that permeated just about every layer of society.

On another level, there is embedded within the KMT an equivalent institution to the GIO, the Department of Cultural Affairs (DCA). According to one former Taiwan newspaper editor, Chen Chiu–kun, the DCA is still more powerful than the GIO, even though it has no legal authority or power. The DCA focused on political affairs and used its extensive network of personal connections to fulfil its responsibilities. Decisions on the media were made only after the DCA, GIO and TGC conferred, with the latter having final authority. Neither the GIO nor the Legislative Yuan were happy with this situation. One editor of an opposition journal remarked: 'The Garrison Command only cares about internal security. They're not responsible for Taiwan's international image or to legislators' (Berman, 1992). After martial law was lifted, the GIO was relegated to attending to the more mundane technical matters associated with publishing and broadcasting, such as licensing (Berman, 1992).

Given such deep and penetrative political supervision, it is not surprising that the first rule of the *Broadcasting and Television Law* declared television's primary purpose to be political service. Television networks were legally required to publicise national policies and public decrees.[16] The KMT identified its own security with their domination of Taiwan, and with the commitment to reunification. These concerns have always taken priority, as demonstrated by the choice of language that television programmes used. In turn, this illustrates how media issues have become politicised and can revolve around the thorny issue of identity, itself posing a significant challenge to the internal security of the ROC.

Under martial law the media in Taiwan were, like the other vehicles for the transmission of political values (for example education), forced to adopt those interpretations of identity that were consistent with the KMT's ideology. Language was an obvious battle–ground. The government preferred to use the term 'dialect' instead of language when referring to Hakka and Taiwanese Hokkien. This has been a deliberate attempt to foster unity among the people on Taiwan and generate a sense of a shared 'Chinese' identity (Lee, 1979). Mandarin became the official language, while Hakka and Hokkien are merely dialects *of* Mandarin.[17] Television celebrated Chinese heroes, while Taiwanese culture was denied a voice within the mainstream media (thus prompting the opposition to seek alternative channels of expression. See Chapter 2). The Taiwanese culture was not suppressed, but confined to the private sphere. In this way the Taiwanese identity was able to survive (Mengin, 1999). The situation prior to 1987 has been best summarised by Thomas B. Gold:

> Although the regime acknowledged that Taiwan had regional particularities, like any other locality in China, the KMT assiduously promoted the idea that the island was the repository and guarantor of Chinese tradition as well as the mainland's rich diversity. ... Popular culture stressed mainland roots, addressing history and life on the island. Politically and to some extent culturally, then, Taiwan became a microcosm of pre–1949 mainland China as interpreted by the KMT (Gold, 1993).

By the 1970s the three national television stations could no longer resist the force of commercial pressure and were thus obliged to use Taiwanese language programmes to compete for ratings (70 per cent of the population spoke Taiwanese). Yet sensing a threat to its definition of security, the government accused these broadcasters of erecting barriers to national unity and the construction of a consistent national identity. In response the stations reduced their Taiwanese programming in 1972 from 50 per cent to less than 20 per cent, and then in 1985 to less than 10 per cent of the total.

By the end of 1988 language became a political issue that yet again pitted Taiwanese against Mainlander. The Hakkas Rights Promotion Union initiated the first Hakka collective social movement since 1949 and launched a campaign that aimed for 'Returning My Mother Tongue'. Their tactics included street protests that demanded television and radio programmes be broadcast in their language. They called for the 'complete liberalization of Hakka radio programming, and the revision of Article 20 of the broadcasting regulations, which limits the use of "dialects" in broadcasting, to support the preservation of these "dialects" and to create a pluralistic and liberalized language policy'.[18] Under pressure the GIO consequently persuaded TTV to broadcast a special programme in Hakka on Sundays in 1989 and, from September 1991 onwards, the three television networks were required to schedule a daily 20 minutes news programme in Hakka (Cheng *et.al*, 1993). The launch of the legal Formosa Hakka Radio in 1996 signalled the end of an era and the beginning of a new bright one for minority language programming (see Chapter 3). That it was able to begin operating was due to revisions made to the restrictions on the use of such languages, passed by the Legislative Yuan in 1993, though the tone remains one of suspicion.

Table 1   **Proportion of Taiwanese programmes shown on the three television stations, 1970–1991 (%)**

	TTV	CTV	CTS
1970	50.00*	47.00	50.00*
1972	17.00	20.00	16.00
1976	10.00	12.00	12.00
1980	12.00	13.00	13.00
1985	8.00	9.00	7.00
1990	8.05	8.00*	9.00*
1991	8.38	8.00*	9.00*

* Estimated

Source: Chin–Chuan Lee (1979: 157 & 1989: 193); Heng Su (1993: 270)

Radio stations broadcasting domestically should primarily use the languages of the nation. This article particularly guarantees the right of broadcast of the languages of ethnic minorities or other minority groups and makes no stipulations about language use ratios'.[19]

Yet the long–term policy against minority languages had already created several complex problems that could not be easily resolved by such minor improvements in programming. Such discrimination has reinforced the arguments voiced by those who use language to define the political and cultural divisions in Taiwan, especially the opposition Democratic Progressive Party (DPP). It is significant that during elections, DPP candidates tend to campaign in Mandarin and Taiwanese, thus attracting votes from their core supporters (during the 1996 Presidential election, all candidates other than the KMT's Lee Teng-hui campaigned in both Mandarin and Taiwanese). Moreover the underground media, together with radio stations and cable television channels that support independence, also use Taiwanese as their principal language. The media that support unification with the mainland prefer to use Mandarin. In this way the opposition believed that Taiwan's security was best preserved by reaffirming the island's indigenous identity. In turn this threatened the position of the KMT that such developments endangered the security of 'Free China' and the prospects of reunification.

So television reflected the KMT's ideas of security. Programmes about politics and public affairs were conservative and uncritical; Taiwan's native culture and traditional arts were discouraged; and most programmes, including news, concentrated overwhelmingly on the interests and life–styles of the metropolitan areas, especially Taipei. In fact many viewers living outside the capital complained that they knew far more about what happened there, and even in the United States, than in their home towns (Kuo, 1990).[20] Although many viewers criticised these programming policies, government support for the television stations meant they were immune to public criticism. The KMT not only enjoyed copious profits from their investment, it seemed clear that entertainment programmes limited public space that might otherwise have been used to challenge the government. Voices of opposition had to discover alternative media channels, as described in the next chapter.

Notes

1.   Dr Sun–Yat Sen is the founder of the KMT and the leader of the 1911 nationalist revolution. The most important strands of Dr Sun's thought are the *Three Principles of the People* which were included in the ROC's constitution. The three principles are nationalism, democracy, and livelihood – government of the people, for the people, by the people.

2.   'By making the power and coherence of the dominant party the chief condition of national survival the party blurs the distinction between the ruling party and the state' (Giliomee & Simkins, 1999).

3.   In 1947, the KMT government of China claimed that 20 million Chinese voted in these elections. 3045 representatives were elected to the National Assembly, all of whom were members of the KMT. Similarly in 1948, 773 were elected the Legislative Yuan. As the ROC moved its capital to Taipei in 1949, all these representatives were transported to Taiwan. Copper (1997); Long (1991); Tien (1989).

4.   'The United States has no predatory design on Formosa [Taiwan] or on any other Chinese territory. The United States has no desire to obtain special rights or privileges, or to establish military bases on Formosa at this time. Nor does it have any intention of utilizing its armed forces to interfere in the present situation. The United States will not pursue a course which will lead to involvement in the civil conflict in China ... Similarly the United States will not provide military aid or advice to Chinese forces on Formosa ...' (Kerr, 1966).

5.   The Korean war interfered with Mao's plans for the invasion of Taiwan. Apparently he ordered several army units to the Taiwan strait only forty–eight hours before North Korea attacked the South. See Gaddis (1997).

6.   In 1958 the shelling of the islands was designed to have more symbolic value than to push the US and Taiwan to the brink of war with China. In fact Zhou Enlai had told the Soviet foreign minister, Andrei Gromyko, that the Chinese did not intend to take either Taiwan or the islands by force (Gaddis, 1997). The purpose of the shelling was to send a clear signal to Washington. The shelling of the islands became central to the PRC's psychological warfare against Taiwan. It had little military value beyond reminding Taipei of Beijing's commitment to 'liberate' Taiwan at some unspecified time in the future (Rawnsley, 2000).

7.   'Taiwanese' refers to the Chinese who have lived in Taiwan since the 16th Century. The largest group are the Min–nan who arrived in Taiwan from southern Fuchien province and speak southern Fuchienese. This book will also make reference to the Hakka, a smaller sub–ethnic group of Taiwanese from Fuchien and Guangdong provinces and speak Hakka. 'Mainlanders' are nationalists who arrived in Taiwan in large numbers after their defeat by the Communists in 1949. Among the most useful accounts are *Common Wealth* (1992), Moody (1995), *The Republic of China on Taiwan Today* (1990) and for a broader historical perspective, Meskill (1979), and Metraux (1991).

8.   It is also worth noting that recent discussions of the Japanese occupation have presented revisionist history of the period. Although far from benevolent, the Japanese were not the tyrannical occupation power in Taiwan that earlier studies have suggested. They were instead crucial to Taiwan's subsequent development. See Lai, Myers & Wei (1991), and Klintworth (1995).

9.   Many useful accounts of 2–28 are available that explore the variety of explanations for the incident. These include Chiou (1995); Kerr (1976); Chiu (1979); Long

(1991); Lai *et.al.*, (1991); Wou (1991); Chen (1992); Ferdinand (1996). Lai *et.al.* (1991) argue against the idea that 2–28 was instigated by the KMT to destroy the native elite. Rather they claim that the outbreak of violence was a surprise to Chen I who had transferred 90 per cent of the Nationalist military out of Taiwan in 1946. Moreover the number of dead far exceeded the size of the native elite.

10.   While mainlanders certainly dominated the KMT, it would be wrong to assume that the party did not also attract a large number of Taiwanese members. By April 1950, the party had recruited only one thousand new Taiwanese members. Two years later, Taiwanese accounted for over half the membership – some 56 per cent (Chao & Myers, 1998).

11.   Pamphlet titled 'DPP' (Taipei, spring 1988).

12.   However, dissident activities against the KMT continued. As Chiou (1995) has observed, these opposition elites 'were not great in number in the 1950s and 1960s, and under the "white terror" of the martial law government of the Nationalists, they could not get much popular support among the severely intimidated Taiwanese people ... Their achievements were not very impressive but they were important in terms of sustaining the opposition campaigns and establishing operational models for the following generations'.

13.   This argument, of course, could be applied to the parts of society: in particular, the 'Taiwan miracle' – economic prosperity and social stability – was used to cushion the blow of martial law and limited democracy.

14.   Chang, C.K., 'Why do we need a public TV station?', *United Daily News*, 14 April 1992.

15.   For further information on the capital and personnel structures of the television companies, see Lee (1979 & 1989); *The Corporation of Broadcasting and Television Enterprise of the ROC* (1990); *Common Wealth* (1991); Cheng *et.al* (1993); C.K. Chiang, 'Expecting the Establishment of a Media Union', *China Times Express*, 18 June 1994; Chang (1994).

16.   Article 1 of the 1976 *Broadcasting and Television Law* (amended in 1982), states: 'This law is enacted to administer and assist radio broadcasting and television enterprises to achieve the purposes of making known national policies and government orders, reporting news, making commentaries, providing decent recreation and enhancing public welfare'.

17.   The authors must acknowledge their debt to Matthew Ward who contributed a stimulating article ('Languages must fight for survival') on the subject of dialects in Taiwan to the *Taipei Times* (28 November 1999).

18.   www.taiwaninfo.org/info/sinorama/en/1998/199812/712094e1.htm

19.   www.taiwaninfo.org/info/sinorama/en/1998/199812/712094e1.htm

20.   From 1 November to 31 December 1992, the stations devoted 27.4 per cent of programme time to news about the central government; 23.3 per cent (news about Taipei); 28.04 per cent (regional news, including Taiwan's provincial government); 19.29 per cent (foreign news); 0.97 per cent (News about mainland China). Chiang (1994).

2 The Media and Popular Protest

'But there exists another, more subversive narrative or set of narratives, according to which democracy has come into being precisely because the masses have dared to speak out and even rebel. Democracy in this view is less a set of institutions than an unfinished emancipatory process, kept in motion by the failure of existing political arrangements ... to assure social justice, protect marginalized groups, and overcome public apathy. Hence it tells a shifting tale of ideals proclaimed and betrayed, struggles won and lost, tyranny and freedom'
– Robinson and White (eds.), (1999).

Introduction

Taiwan has a long tradition of powerful and vocal media that present a challenge to government strength. Descriptions of the political system – including our own, presented in the previous chapter – have tended to focus on the authoritarian character of KMT governance. Yet when we delve below such superficial analyses we instantly discover the extent to which this same government realised that it was necessary to tolerate a modicum of press freedom. The critical or opposition media provided a non–violent form of opposition, and helped to reinforce the ROC's legitimacy as 'Free China', an image that was especially powerful in its diplomacy with the US (Rawnsley 2000a & 2000c).

During the long period of martial law that began in 1949 the government of the ROC shouldered responsibility for setting the boundaries of what could be expressed in the media. Ambiguity was found at the margins where the commercial demands of the market clashed with political responsibility (Lee, 1999). The media often found themselves in the difficult position of trying to maximise audience share by giving them what they wanted, while fulfilling the political role they were expected to play by the KMT. Permissible (and encouraged) criticism included any that held the day-to-day administration accountable for their actions. If the media openly challenged the KMT's ideology, its political monopoly, or its goal of eventually recovering the mainland, or if they advocated independence, then they had crossed the boundaries, and their activities could be classified as illegal. To illustrate this we can turn to the spheres of consensus, legitimate controversy and unacceptable controversy that Daniel Hallin developed to ease our understanding of the American media's position on the Vietnam War. Diagram 1 shows how the spheres relate to each other, and then demonstrates their applicability to the situation in Taiwan.

Figure 1   Hallin's spheres and their applicability to Taiwan

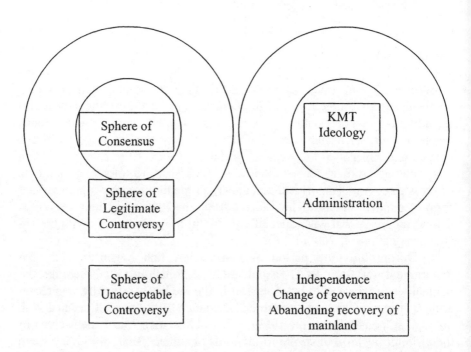

Source: Adapted from Hallin (1986)

The 'sphere of consensus' is here presented as a sacrosanct area that embraces the KMT's ideology. Thus acceptance of the KMT's monopoly on central power, the eventual reunification of the Chinese mainland on the KMT's terms, and the concept of Taiwan as merely a province of China, all lay within this sphere. This framework corresponds to the 'four implicit rules' that Chou and Myers identified as 'delineating the boundary between acceptable and unacceptable political behaviour' as defined by the KMT. These rules 'defined the structural relationship between society and the political centre' during the long period of political tutelage, that is, for as long as the government decided that Taiwan was not prepared to embrace democracy and that the communist threat prevented the realisation of the Three Principles of the People:

- Adjusting the 1947 constitution to the political realities of Taiwan to make it the basis for law, authority, and political legitimation
- Preserving the single–party rule of the KMT through martial law but allowing two client parties to exist: the Young China Party (YCP) and the China Democratic Socialist Party (CDSP)
- Promoting 'limited democracy' in Taiwan province by allowing for elections of local government assemblies and offices and eventually (1969) limited numbers of national representatives
- Permitting the competition of ideas while not tolerating Marxism, Leninism, socialist thought, or criticisms likely to delegitimize the political center (Chou & Myers, 1998)

The 'sphere of legitimate controversy' allows and encourages criticism. In Taiwan's case this meant acceptable criticism of the day-to-day administration of the island and, from 1950 onwards, limited electoral competition at the local level.[1] Entry to the 'sphere of unacceptable controversy' means that the permitted boundaries have been crossed. Here we find discussion of ideas that contradict the sphere of consensus, i.e. the KMT's ideology: the KMT's monopoly on government is challenged; the relegation of the Taiwanese identity to the private sphere is questioned, as is the necessity of a prolonged state of martial law; and Taiwan's independence and sovereignty are advocated. Press freedom was permitted in all spheres except the sphere of unacceptable controversy. This therefore became the realm dominated by the opposition and underground media that challenged the KMT and sought to mobilise their audience around a radical political agenda.

The government of the ROC was responsible for determining which issues fell within each of the spheres, and was thus answerable for what could be expressed in the media. For example the government found it convenient to overlook the divisions within the opposition, especially over the issue of Taiwan's independence from China (Arrigo, 1981; Chen, 1982; Domes, 1981; T'ang, 1979). Some critics of the KMT remained committed to both democracy *and* the eventual unification with China,[2] though such complexities could not provide the easy packaging sought by KMT propaganda. The party maintained that opposing the KMT equated with advocating independence and subverting national security, and this provided the framework of political discourse until the late 1980s. The KMT–dominated media used a rich vocabulary to berate opposition activists who broke the law: they were classified in Chinese as different forms of criminals – *baotu* ('violent character'), *bufu fenzi* ('illegal individual'), *yexin fenzi* ('politically ambitious individual') – who were unable to distinguish right from wrong and lacked any sense of definable morality. Ultimately they were a threat to Taiwan's security, the ultimate justification of suppression against which no one could easily argue (Chou & Myers, 1998). Such vocabulary made it absolutely clear that the opposition was located within the sphere of unacceptable controversy and therefore outside the realms of social and political toleration.

Although the *China Times* (*Zhongguo Shi pao*) and the *United Daily News* (*Lien ho pao*), Taiwan's two newspapers with the largest market–share of readers,[3] were required to support the government (they were after all founded in the early 1950s by two mainlanders with close ties to the KMT), they still found themselves subject to market forces. These privately owned newspapers were therefore driven by market competition to be as innovative and independent as regulations would allow. Political and business interests frequently clashed, and the press often deviated from the official position. This would often mean they could criticise the government provided they did not discuss issues that lay in the sphere of unacceptable controversy (Tien, 1989). They therefore operated within *both* the spheres of consensus and legitimate controversy. This was in stark contrast to the newspapers that were *directly* owned and/or controlled by the KMT or state agencies. They were unable to venture beyond the sphere of consensus.

The relationship between the government and the media is best illustrated by reference to the Cultural Clearance Campaign, launched in 1954. Newspapers were prohibited from publishing stories about a wide range of issues – from teenage crime, to sex, gambling and drug abuse. However, the list also included several vague prohibitions: The press should refrain from publishing reports about political, military and foreign affairs that may damage the national interest; and they were instructed not to report anything that 'insulted' the leadership, or affected the reputation of the government. So not only had the sphere of legitimate controversy contracted at the government's behest, thus expanding the sphere of unacceptable controversy, but also the authorities enjoyed tremendous latitude in terms of how these regulations could be defined and interpreted.[4] The privately owned press mobilised and collectively protested against these restrictions on their work. After only five days the Executive Yuan backed down and decided to suspend the regulations. The newspaper industry claimed a moral and political victory. However, it was not to last. Similar protests in 1958 against the ostensibly secret passage of the Publication Laws through the Legislative Yuan failed. The owner of the *Independent Evening Post (Zeli Wanpao)*, Lee Yu-je, resigned from the KMT and declared his newspapers to be *'Wutan Wupai'* – 'No Party, No Faction'. Together with *'Duli Jingying'* ('Independent Management'), these remain the rallying cries of the *Independent Evening Post* (Chen & Chu, 1987). The *Post* quickly acquired a reputation as one of the few newspapers in Taiwan not to blindly follow the KMT line.

While the mainstream press had their own differences of opinion with the KMT government, they could never challenge the state apparatus in any meaningful way. The opposition press, on the other hand, were not so constrained, and they had another far more valuable political function than simply relaying news and views. These newspapers and journals provided a training ground for activists, eager to learn the arts of political participation, competition and mobilisation. In this way the opposition press performed many of the same functions of traditional political parties: they provided the movement with ideological direction, opportunities for patronage, the aggregation of interests, and the recruitment and training of leaders (Berman, 1992).[5] Daniel Berman believes that the opposition press were more interested in these functions – forming a surrogate political party – than simply disseminating views and opinions.

> By continually pushing – and subsequently expanding – the limits of acceptable behaviour, by providing a non–violent, legal context in which a de facto opposition could develop and mature, opposition magazine organisations made a substantial contribution to the relatively smooth transition to a much more democratic form of government (Berman, 1992).

They also created and shaped the identities that would coalesce around the opposition movement to the present, that is, representation of the poor, the working class, and most importantly, the Taiwanese. What the authorities could never quite understand, was that through these media the opposition movement was merely demanding what was provided for in the constitution – meaningful elections and the right to organise alternative political parties.

The Rise of the Opposition, 1947–1977

Although the KMT has permitted electoral contestation on Taiwan – albeit only at the local level – since 1950, elections were essentially non–competitive. Competition occurred only between factions of the KMT. The fate of the Taiwanese leaders after the February 28 incident has already been noted. Thus organised opposition to the KMT was non–existent on Taiwan. Instead the nucleus of social movements that challenged the government were found in the United States and Japan. Some leaders had fled there during the 'White Terror' of the early 1950s, others had been sent there in exile. Several independent candidates did challenge the KMT's hegemony in elections and were successful. Critics were allowed to hold public meetings and sit in judgement over the regime provided such behaviour did not threaten the party–state rule over Taiwan. However, such activities were tolerated only because they presented no major threat to the party and because they strengthened the projection abroad of the ROC as a free and democratic political system.[6] Involvement in elections provided a useful training ground for activists, many of whom would in time become leading figures in the opposition movement (even Presidential contenders). Eventually, a velvet revolution occurred:

> A political opposition gradually emerged and skillfully expanded its political influence, and the ruling party gradually learned how to tolerate and live with the political opposition. The evolutionary phase of limited democracy was crucial for Taiwan's democratic breakthrough and consolidation because it provided enough time for the people and elites to 'learn democracy by practicing it' and for their political cultural values to become conducive to the practice of democracy (Chao & Myers, 1998).

Hence the brutality of the government's response to 2–28 could not completely silence its critics. The political opposition learned to use short–lived, though powerful and inspirational political magazines or journals to consolidate their ideas and mobilisation. Daniel K. Berman has done most to add to our awareness of these magazines, and he allows us to understand why this specific medium was preferred over all others. First, newspapers were difficult to establish and operate under KMT regulations. They had to be licensed, and they were governed by strict guidelines that restricted the number of pages that could be printed. Magazines were not subject to such harsh treatment. In addition, magazines required less start–up capital, they could function according to irregular publishing schedules, and they were more durable than newspapers. These factors made them suitable for underground production and distribution (Berman, 1992).

The political magazines were at the forefront of the first attempt to create a credible alternative to the KMT. *Public Opinion News* (*Gounlun Pao*, established in October 1947) and *Free China Fortnightly* (*Ziyou Zhongguo*, established November 1949) were the earliest dissident media in Taiwan. *Free China Fortnightly* provided the inspiration behind the creation of the China Democratic Party in 1960. The magazine was launched in 1949 with subsidies from the government and the Ministry of Education as part of their liberal challenge to communism. It's co–founder was Lei Chan, a prominent KMT minister without portfolio and an adviser to the Office of the President. Although a committed party cadre, Lei earned the wrath of colleagues when, during the 1950s, he pressed for a more discernible separation of the party and the military. Typical of the editorials it published was one headlined 'The government should not lure people into crime,' intended as a critique of a corruption case among intelligence officers. Many, including Chiang Kai–shek and Chiang Ching–kuo, accused him of communist sympathies and placed him under close surveillance. Lei believed that 'single party authoritarian rule' was responsible for the KMT's defeat on the mainland, and that free discussion and criticism within the party might have stymied its failures. He called for the government to guarantee civil liberties and create a political system that included effective checks and balances. Only then would the KMT be strong enough to compete with the communists.

By 1956 *Free China Fortnightly* had refocused its attention on internal problems and became increasingly critical of corruption, constitutional violations, and the absence of multi–party politics in Taiwan. In short, this journal and others like it demanded merely what was provided for in the constitution. The editorials in the *Free China Fortnightly* assumed a more acerbic tone: 'We have tolerated too much for the unity of the war against Communism. This in turn has led to an embrace of one party politics and hampers the path towards progress.' The journal warned that if the KMT, which 'selfishly, for the sake of its own interests is not willing to accept conditions of equality' with competing opinions should ignore such demands, then there was 'no hope at the present for democratic government in China. In that case the only recourse is to wait for the next revolution! Let more blood flow!' (Berman, 1992). Editorials advocated the creation of a loyal opposition movement, the China Democratic Party, to promote electoral reform:

> I hope that everyone who believes in democratic politics will gather to form an opposition party in order to break the monopoly of the KMT. The rationale for a new party is that it must gain political authority by competing in elections. Our constitution (Article 14) empowers individuals with the freedom to form a party. This new opposition party can be organised immediately, but it must be protected by the law (Chao & Myers, 1998).

Yet these were stirring words that suggested to the KMT the possibility of an internal revolution against them. In 1955 Lei Chan was expelled from the KMT, after which he was placed under surveillance, his telephone conversations were monitored and his letters were opened. In September 1960 he was arrested and stood accused on various counts of sedition that included: associating with communists; denying the possibility of recovering the mainland; urging the United States to interfere in the internal affairs of the ROC; encouraging divisions between the government and military; helping communist 'United Front' tactics in Taiwan; and promoting the partition of mainlanders and Taiwanese. Lei was sentenced to ten years in prison and the China Democratic Party was destroyed at its conception.[7]

The owner of *Public Opinion News*, Lee Wan–ju, faced similar ill fate. In 1959 Lee also planned to organise a new political party, but constant government harassment and the repeated confiscation of printing facilities made *Public Opinion News* vulnerable to severe financial problems. However, the ultimate dissolution of Lee's press empire was not caused by blatant political or judicial interference, but by the KMT's decision to invest enormous sums in *Public Opinion News*. Once they enjoyed a controlling interest, it was easy for the KMT to engineer the journal's downfall. Lee was forced out of business by the skilful manipulation of investment concerns, not by government pressure (Fang, 1995).

One of the most influential magazines of the pre-reform era was the *Taiwan Political Review* (*Taiwan zhenglun*), created in 1975 by Kang Ning–hsiang. Advocating free and open debate about any issues that the people of Taiwan felt the need to discuss, and demanding greater Taiwanese involvement in the political life of the island, the *Review* highlighted the injustices and extra–constitutional nature of the political system. Again, the journal intended to provide the basis for a substantive political movement. Thus Kang 'introduced a model of the opinion magazine that could be used to work towards change within the system, building a political party apparatus that could eventually emerge at a proper time, fully formed, from the recesses of its journalistic cover to smooth the transition to a democratic political system' (Berman, 1992). By its fifth issue, the circulation of the *Review* had peaked at 50,000 with 2,000 subscribers abroad, although these are conservative estimates; we can never know for sure exactly how many read the journal as it circulated. We owe to the *Review* the term *tangwai* to refer to political activists outside the KMT ('a new party without a formal title[8]). Such labelling had immense symbolic significance for it provided a sense of cohesion to the opposition movement. Its most vociferous writer, Huang Hua, despaired of the subdued character of his people: 'To be afraid of politics and the KMT is a widespread pathology our society,' he wrote. Huang described how, although the KMT had committed many serious errors, 'it never feared being ejected from office or being violently overthrown because the people of Taiwan were cowed by it' (Chao & Myers, 1998). By the end of 1975, the *Review* was closed down, and Huang and his colleagues were arrested.

Other journals appeared, such as *China Tide* (*Xia Chao*), a socialist publication that from July 1976 to January 1979 advocated reunification with the mainland, criticised the domination of foreign capital in Taiwan, and generally campaigned for social welfare rights for peasants and workers; and *This Generation* (*Je Yidai*), organised by former staff of the *Taiwan Political Review*, and renamed *Great Virtue* after it was suspended. The October 1977 issue was accused of having violated the law and was sentenced to close down for one year (Fang, 1995).

Transformation: 1977–1986

With the accession of Chiang Ching–kuo to the presidency in 1978 following a brief interregnum after his father's death in 1975, the conditions were in place to ensure Taiwan's political system would keep pace with its dynamic economy. During his life, Ching-kuo had been anything but a democrat, but he did realise that the international shocks required the ROC to discard its authoritarian political system. As premier and chairman of the KMT he recruited Taiwanese into the party and government, thus launching the 'Taiwanisation' of the ROC that would enable Taiwan–born Lee Teng–hui to succeed him as President (Cheng & Haggard, 1992). A populist, Ching–kuo championed anti–corruption at all layers of the government, and sought to make the state more responsive to public opinion.

The late 1970s were marked by a number of external shocks that had widespread internal repercussions. The political opposition discovered renewed hope with the election of Jimmy Carter to the US Presidency and his platform that expressed a genuine concern for human rights throughout the world.   Yet his decision to fully normalise relations with the PRC, together with renewed economic competition with the mainland to corner the export market during a global recession that for a time seemed to threaten the Taiwan economic miracle, reinforced the KMT's determination to hold on to power. The state could again justify this by claiming it had the island's security at heart, but it had little effect. The government's muted response to, and management of, changes in the external environment 'hammered away at its legitimacy in the eyes of its citizenry' (Gold, 1986).   Government legitimacy was further eroded when the national supplementary elections, scheduled for December 1978, were cancelled. This was a major set-back for the *tangwai* who had appeared to be heading for a landmark victory, but only the *Formosa* faction decided to protest, thus ripping apart the opposition movement even further. However, America's move and the KMT's response, the emerging democracy movement in the PRC (quickly suppressed once it had served the interests of the leadership. See Baum, 1994), and even the success of the Iranian revolution, all emboldened the *tangwai*.   President Chiang's 'Taiwanisation' of the ROC had held open the opportunity for greater ethnic diversity in the political process. It had also nullified the opposition that had previously mobilised its support along ethnic cleavages, and would eventually pacify those who defined politics in Taiwan with reference to national identity. The *Formosa* faction believed that the climate was now ripe to press harder for expanded political involvement. Twenty years on, the leaders of the movement would suggest they were concerned with Taiwan's security in light of the normalisation of relations between the US and China:

> In the past, the US – which led the fight against Communism – supported Taiwan wholeheartedly. But this was no longer the case after its decision to consider detente with Beijing. We realised it was time to reconsider Taiwan's future from our own viewpoint, instead of allowing the KMT to be the only decision maker for the island's destiny (Shih Ming-teh, quoted in the *Taipei Times*, 9 December 1999).

In 1977, a young Taiwanese politician by the name of Hsu Hsin–liang ran as an independent in the election for magistrate of Taoyuan County. Under Chiang Ching–kuo's commitment to expanding opportunities for native Taiwanese to enter government service, he had already served one term as a member of the KMT, but he had angered his party colleagues by straying from the official line. The party therefore decided he should not run for a second term. In the election Hsu lost to his KMT opponent. This provoked strong public protest in the county town of Chungli where the governing party was accused of electoral fraud. According to one observer, this was the largest public demonstration of its kind since 1947:

> In the face of this public display the regime backed down and admitted that there had indeed been fraud. Hsu was re-elected. The Chungli incident marked a change of atmosphere, a toleration for active and outspoken political dissent (Moody, 1995).

Despite his popularity and victory in the election, Hsu was still dismissed from office by the central government in June 1979. This was a response to his lead in an anti–KMT demonstration in Chiaotou which, the Control Yuan alleged, had compromised his official position. Hsu mobilised his supporters and launched a new political journal, *Formosa* (*Meilitao*) on 16 August 1979. This was a more radical publication than any of its predecessors that had merely challenged the KMT to reform the system. *Formosa* went further, and committed the cardinal sin of calling for Taiwan's independence and direct popular confrontation with the government. Articles complained that the government arbitrarily closed down critical journals, whether they were communist, subversive, or neither; called for a complete reform of the National Assembly; and criticised the rather haphazard commitment to the democratic vision of the Three Principles of the People. These facts were widely advertised in another journal, *Current Monthly* (*Nuanliu zazhi*) in a lively 1984 article by Chen Yanghao entitled 'Prohibit! Prohibit! Prohibit!' (*'Jin! Jin! Jin'*):

> KMT's censorship policy was everywhere in society and for no explicable reason the KMT prohibited every kind of behaviour: it forbade any revision of the constitution before recovering the mainland; it forbade any new party from forming; it forbade the registration of any newspaper; it forbade strike, demonstrations, and criticisms of national policy; it forbade the election of a provincial governor and the mayors of Taipei and Kaohsiung cities; it forbade the reading of works published by mainland Chinese authors; it forbade the expression of views by political rallies; it forbade students to have long hair and to help politicians in elections. Most of these activities do not violate the constitution. They are merely the subjective views held by those in power and run counter to society's contemporary trends and the natural inclinations of our people.

Such subjective views determined how the government would react to *Formosa*. The popularity of the journal at first astonished and then frightened the government who had allowed the magazine to circulate. The crunch came when the activists behind the magazine began to organise political meetings throughout Taiwan that attracted thousands in attendance. A series of rallies and demonstrations ended spectacularly in Kaohsiung on 10 December 1979 (to coincide with Human Rights Day), a few days before elections to the Legislative Yuan were scheduled to take place. The police were called to prevent the group from congregating (permission to meet had been denied), and a riot ensued after *Formosa* publications were seized by police, and activists severely beaten while in custody. As C.L. Chiou has observed: 'The 'Formosa' affair ... was a mass organisation, a political institution, with many salient party characteristics offering a clear and credible threat to the authoritarian power of the ruling KMT ... That, the Nationalist government was not prepared to tolerate' (Chiou, 1995).[9]

Bowing to both international and domestic pressures, the government was required to hold trials for those involved in the 'Formosa' incident in an open military court.[10]   The mass media, including the three national television stations, were permitted to report the procedures and to cover in full the speeches made by the defence lawyers. Fearing for their safety, very few attorneys step forwards to represent the defendants. Among those who did choose to take such risks included Chen Shui–bian who, in 1994 was elected the DPP mayor of Taipei and as Taiwan's president in 2000. Hsu Hsin–liang was found guilty and sentenced to exile in the United States.[11] Seven other 'Formosa' leaders were sentenced to between twelve years and life imprisonment, while more than sixty others were sentenced to a mere three to eight years in prison. The president of *Formosa* Shih Ming–teh, the DPP's presidential candidate in 1996 and after the party chairman, was imprisoned from 1980 to 1990 for his part in the incident. Lin Yi–hsiung, at the time a member of the provincial assembly, was imprisoned for four years. At the time of writing, he is the Chairman of the DPP. Annette Lu, elected Chen Shui–bian's Vice–President in 2000 also stood accused in 1979. Their defence lawyers addressed human rights issues and alluded in their speeches to the principles of law and democracy. Because the trials received such intense media attention, such orations reached a wide audience. Thus although 'the KMT did manage to win the legal battles,' notes Chiou, 'they certainly failed to convince the Taiwanese people and to win a moral–political victory. Overnight, the 'Formosa' defendants became political martyrs whose martyrdom would continue to haunt the KMT regime up to the present day' (Chiou, 1995).

When the political dissidents were expelled to the US, the *tangwai* movement spread abroad with them. Hsu Hsin–liang continued to write and publish passionate articles advocating the overthrow of the KMT government. He went so far as to suggest in the 1982 issues of *Formosa* (now published in the US) that the only way Taiwan would throw off KMT domination was by engaging in urban guerrilla warfare against the government. Hsu even went so far as to introduce the translation of a Cuban guerrilla terrorist manual – a move guaranteed to draw him to the attention of the US government.

Back in Taiwan, the *Independent Evening Post* continued to act as a thorn in the KMT's side. Editorials contested decisions to arrest prominent dissidents, while reports covered human rights issues, political repression, and the rise of the *tangwai*. One of the most famous stories that the *Post* covered was Hsu Hsin–liang's proposed return to Taiwan. On 29 November 1986, Hsu left New York for Tokyo, a flight that involved a scheduled refuelling stop in Taipei. On 1 December, some two thousand people congregated at the Chiang Kai–shek International Airport in Taoyuan to greet him. Violence broke out when the military and airport police tried to disperse the crowd. As water hoses and tear gas were turned on the people, three policemen were injured (Chen & Chu, 1987).[12] For the KMT–controlled press, this incident justified the continuation of martial law: how could the government tolerate the existence of a group of subversives who used violence to achieve their objectives? The press reported that support for the DPP had fallen, and in the subsequent elections, reminded voters that the party 'fomented violence at the Taoyuan international airport'. Only the *Independent Evening Post* reported that the police had started the violence. The DPP were anxious to tell their side of the story, and showed video footage in public to reinforce it (Li, 1991).

The *Independence Evening Post* again found itself the focus of political attention when, in September 1987, two reporters obtained visas in Japan to visit the PRC. As circulation soared the editor in chief, Wu Fengshan, and the two reporters themselves were indicted for 'filing false documents'. They were all acquitted by the Taipei District Court in April 1988. The *Post* offered readers a radical alternative of news and information from the style of reporting offered by other newspapers.[13]

Now, however, the opposition movement itself had split between those who sought to overthrow KMT domination by further radical action on the streets of Taiwan, and those who deemed it necessary to use legal parliamentary channels to undermine the system from within. As the factions within the movement grew, the competition between the journals and magazines intensified. In turn their credibility was often damaged.

Financial pressure and commercial competition forced many magazines to provide titillation – to expose special and otherwise secret 'facts' that had little basis in truth. And as the credibility of the magazines was suspect, the reputation of the whole *tangwai* movement that they supported was discredited. By the mid–1980s, the relevance of the magazines began to fade and videos, produced and distributed underground by members of the opposition became much more common. The opposition had discovered the convenience and value of the electronic media, and the so–called '5–20' incident in 1980 demonstrated just how important such videos had become.

Feeling that their rights had been neglected by the government for long enough, 5,000 farmers from the central and southern parts of Taiwan staged in May 1988 a demonstration in Taipei.[14] Sadly the protests turned to violence, with more than one hundred protesters being arrested. The press and the three national television stations all portrayed the incident as a 'riot', a term resonant with political significance. Their news reports were full of images of an hysterical public attacking the Legislative Yuan, parked cars being set on fire, policemen wounded by flying stones, and the streets of Taipei in chaos.[15] *The China Times* buried reports in the back pages, choosing to downplay the street protests rather than being forced to take sides. However, the *China Times* decided to not live up to its liberal image, and instead voiced the same fear of social and political chaos and reluctance to criticise the military or police that could be found in conservative society.

Perturbed by the images of the riots as threats to security, two small private organisations, the Green Group (*Luse Xiaozu*) and the Third Image (*Disan Yinxian*), captured visual records of the incident on camcorder and edited them into short factual documentaries. Both tapes suggested that the police and army were responsible for the riot by attacking innocent protestors. The tone of the video emphasised a peaceful demonstration, attended by people determined to exercise their democratic rights in standing up to authority and being brutally suppressed for doing so.

The quality of the camcorders could not compete with the professional television cameras, while some of the images were deliberately blurred by the producers to avoid the possibility of their being used as evidence. Moreover, the GIO classified as illegal all the programmes produced by the Green Group and the Third Image, and thus prevented them from being sold, rented, or broadcast in public. The videos did, however, find their way on to the black market where they were widely available and became very popular (Tun *et al.*, 1992). The popularity of the black market versions of the videos implied that the people of Taiwan were eager to seek alternative versions of political events. Clearly, they did not trust the coverage of politics offered by the three national television stations. This explains why the KMT's Department of Cultural Affairs felt obliged to later produce and distribute another video that contained re–edited news material gathered by TTV, CTV and CTS. Although this single official account of the incident recounted the identical story to the three stations, it did at least mean that the KMT government had sensed the pressure generated by this movement against the mainstream electronic media and felt that it had to respond.

So, during the mid–1980s, the electronic media replaced journals, magazines and, to some extent, newspapers, as the main communication channels for the opposition movement. Several independent and illegal video producers, including the Green Group, the Third Image, and New Taiwan, began to disseminate their own electronic versions of the underground journals. Between 1986 and 1988, the above three companies produced between 50 and 60 videos, covering DPP rallies and election campaigns, street protests, parliamentary confrontations, and appeals to particular issues (the environment, for example). But eventually the popularity of these videos likewise faded. Not only did the KMT begin to crack down on the organisation of social movements, but the production companies themselves were forced out of business by competition from the pirate market. However, the most significant limit to their activity was the most simple: restrictions on the press were abolished in 1988. Now it was cheaper and more convenient to obtain one's news from newspapers. The videos had championed the course of press freedom and liberalisation within the industry. Once this was achieved, they were forced out of business (Tun *et.al*, 1992).

Conclusions

Most journalists in Taiwan, whether they represented the mainstream press or the opposition magazines, embraced the norms of their profession and the idea that they had a duty to serve as a check on government activities. Many of the more idealistic journalists from the mainstream press, usually against their editors' wishes, contributed to the poorly staffed and poorly financed *tangwai* magazines the bulk of critical stories that their own journals were prohibited from publishing. It is important to remember that the KMT remained committed to the constitutional provisions for democracy and press freedom, and only argued that these should be suspended *temporarily* in the interest of anti-Communism. The KMT accused such political journals as *Formosa, China Tide, Eighties* and others, of jeopardising national security, and exaggerating the social division between mainlander and Taiwanese. Nevertheless, the opposition challenged as illegal the extra-constitutional network that bound together state, party, and media. They believed that it was their duty to highlight the inconsistency in the government's logic, between the promise to promote democracy and the harsh reality of martial law. In this way, the *tangwai* hoped to erode the legitimacy of the KMT and mobilise the people of Taiwan (especially voters) to support their agenda for reform. The *tangwai* had developed their own form of media – first journals, then videos, always produced and distributed underground – until a twist of irony dealt them a death blow: the achievement of the political reform, social liberalisation, and freedom of speech that they had championed for over three decades put them out of business. They were deprived of their raison d'être. Now, the media that gains the trust of audiences, and thus captures the largest share of the market, are those that perform as 'objective' and 'professional' journalists rather than tools of any one political party. This explains the closure of the *Capital Morning Post* and other opposition magazines. The *Capital Morning Post* had voiced a radical agenda in its editorials, though its reporting was rather more pedestrian. Editorials published on the first anniversary of the 5–20 incident criticised the National Security Law that had replaced martial law in 1987. They therefore argued that street protests were a legitimate means for a people denied constitutional protection to declare their rights. Arbitrary repression by the government would remain a major obstacle to the creation of a truly democratic society. Its news reports, however, were more circumspect, praising the police for their restraint and tolerance in the peaceful protests that marked the anniversary of 5–20 (*Capital Morning Post*, 19 May 1989). Clearly the *Capital Morning Post* was divided politically, undermining the coherence that might otherwise have made it a survivor in the press industry. The lack of a clear identity made it vulnerable to both government and market pressure. In the end, it was simply not as professional as its competitors. As Irena Maryniak observed in 1992: 'In economic conditions where only the most down–market publications can survive without outside support, journalistic compromise frequently becomes a necessity' (Randall, 1993).

Social movements and street protests died down during the 1990s (though they were revived in the immediate aftermath of the 2000 election when disaffected members of the KMT clashed with riot police in Taipei). Liberalisation, combined with a thriving economy that serves the middle classes, have responded to the demands of the increasingly plural civil society. Problems remained to the end of the decade: the separation of state and party was insufficiently clear, with many questions about the neutrality of the judicial and national security agencies still unanswered (Giliomee & Simkins, 1999). Meanwhile corruption and factionalism continue to influence local elections. Taiwan is moving slowly, but inexorably towards democratic consolidation. Cable television has stolen the thunder of the previously dissident media and is responding to the increasingly localised and diverse society that is Taiwan.

Notes

1. For further details see Chao & Myers (1998), p.43.
2. One prominent critic of the KMT who was also against independence was Yu Dengfa, a former ward chief, member of the National Assembly, and three times magistrate of Kaohsiung district. In a 1978 interview, he said: 'I feel that regarding the Taiwan independence issue ... it is not possible. We are all Chinese, and it is only right that China is unified. If someone advocates Taiwan independence, I believe they cannot obtain the endorsement of the international community and they will merely disgrace themselves.' Wang To, *Tangwai di shengyin* (1978, p.37), quoted in Chou & Myers (1998).
3. The *China Times* and *United Daily News* were often referred to as 'The Big Two' as, through corporate consolidation they eventually controlled two–thirds of the island's circulation and press advertising.
4. This vagueness was reflected in the national criminal code (Article 100 of the constitution) that regulated 'domestic criminal violence'. Essentially this Article stated that 'if any person behaves as if he or she *intends* to destroy the national polity, steal or take over national property, use illegal means to change the nation's constitution, or actually carries out these intentions, then that person has committed a crime of domestic criminal violence' (Chao & Myers, 1998).
5. Berman uses Samuel Huntington's (1965) functions of party organisation as his model.
6. In 1968, the KMT government introduced a supplementary type of election to fill vacancies in the seats assigned to Taiwan every three years. After 1972, these limited elections occurred on a regular basis. The number of additional seats created for these elections increased from 51 in the Legislative Yuan and 53 in the National Assembly in 1972, to 101 in the Legislative Yuan in 1989 and 84 in the National Assembly in 1986. The membership of the Control Yuan also increased from 15 in 1972 to 32 in 1987 (Tsang, 1993).
7. Lei continued to press for political reform after he was released from prison. In January 1972, he submitted a 10,000–character petition to Chiang Kai–shek outlining ten areas in need of urgent reform. These included using the word 'Taiwan' in the official name of the country to declare independence.
8. Shih Ming–teh in the *Taipei Times*, 9 December 1999.
9. A full account of the 'Kaohsiung incident' can be found in Chou & Myers, 1997, pp.57-9.
10. Groucho Marx once quipped, 'military justice is to justice what military music is to music'. We are grateful to Brian Kennedy (*Taipei Times*, 19 October 1999) for providing this apt quotation.

11.   Hsu was visiting the US when rioting broke out in Kaohsiung. He did not return to Taiwan to stand trial. He therefore escaped imprisonment, but was unable to return from the US.

12.   In 1987, Hsu sneaked ashore back to Taiwan, but was imprisoned for illegal entry, though released shortly afterwards. Having resigned from the DPP, Hsu was an independent candidate in the 2000 election for President of Taiwan. Hsu came fourth out of five candidates, having secured 0.63 per cent of the vote (79,429 votes).

13.   The *Independent Evening Post* was also the first newspaper to publisher the new constitution of the ROC, drafted by leading dissident Lin Yi-hsiong.

14.   The farmers' grievances had deep roots. The main explanation for this particular protest, organised by the Yunlin Farmers Rights Promotion Union, was the government's effort to acquire Most Favoured Nation status from the United States. This prompted the Legislative Yuan to loosen restrictions on the importation of fruit and vegetables. The farmers worried about the impact this would have on their livelihoods.

15.   The confrontation began at around 3pm and continued well past midnight. It was marked by long periods of stand-off between the farmers and police, rather than continuous violence. This illustrates the power that was attached to the media portrait of the incident as a 'riot'. University students joined the farmers and staged a sit-down protest. However, this only made the situation more chaotic that it already was. One of the DPP's legislators, Chu Kao-cheng, was in the crowd and was accidentally injured after his attempt to negotiate with the police failed. For the next three years, this day was commemorated in a variety of non-violent ways by the opposition movements. Further information can be found in Lin (1991), and Liu (1995).

3 Television and Democratisation

'In blunt terms, money and power tend to be indifferent with respect to cultural diversity'
– Peter Dahlgren (1995).

Taiwan has come a long way since the death in April 1975 of its patriarch, Generalissimo Chiang Kai–shek. His son and eventual heir, Chiang Ching–kuo, was pressured by the changing domestic and international environments detailed in the previous chapter to sweep away the political system that his father had built. Among his greatest achievements was the recruitment of Taiwanese into the KMT and government, the so–called 'Taiwanisation' of the ROC: 'The old division of labor [sic], whereby KMT mainlanders ran national politics and enforced their will while Taiwanese made money in business and channelled their political ambitions into local contests, was breaking down' (Gold, 1986):

> Democratic reform was clearly in the Kuomintang's political self–interest: it provided a further point of contrast with mainland China; it helped broaden the Kuomintang's domestic political base and it was certain to win the approval of influential political bodies in the United States (Klintworth, 1995).

We are reminded, moreover, that reformers rationalised Taiwan's democratisation by expressing their hopes for political change in China. In 1985 Shaw Yu–ming, for example, predicted that:

> China's modernisation would produce a kind of revolution of rising expectations which would seriously shake the political and ideological foundations of the communist government, so much so that for its survival, the Chinese people and their communist leaders will have to look for other models of state building and government administration (Klintworth, 1995).

This preceded the launch in 1987 of a 'political offensive' against the mainland that intended to provoke a democratic revolution against communism. The idea was to demonstrate to the mainland (and the world) that the Chinese were, after all, capable of democracy. The role of the media was in promoting these democratic processes in the mainland and copying the 'contagion' effects of democratisation that characterised many of the revolutions of the late 1980s and early 1990s (Rawnsley, 2000).

Chiang Ching–kuo also launched an anti–corruption drive that propelled many of his own associates from power and into jail, and he won renewed respect at home and abroad as a populist reformer. In 1984 he chose as his Vice President a native Taiwanese, Lee Teng–hui (*The Republic of China on Taiwan Today,* 1990). While this marked the beginning of the transition of power from mainland Chinese to Taiwanese, it would also split the KMT in two, provoking many senior 'old guard' members who were critical of Lee to branch out on their own and, in August 1993 form the New Party (Ferdinand, ed. 1996).[1]

At a landmark meeting of the KMT Central Committee in 1986, President Chiang launched the major political restructuring of the ROC that would change it forever. This included the abolition of martial law and the legalisation of opposition parties (by 1992, there were sixty–three legal political parties. Tsang, ed. 1993). Democracy would still be limited, however, by the National Security Law that still prohibited new political parties from advocating communism or Taiwan's independence (Long, 1991). Clearly Taiwan's security was still threatened during a possibly extensive phase of political transition.

Chiang Ching–kuo died in January 1988 and power transferred to Lee. Lee was committed to realising the political vision of his late mentor, including a thorough reform of the institutions of government to make them more responsive. In April 1991 Lee finally abolished the far from Temporary Provisions of the Constitution that had lingered in the post–martial law period, and the first 'free' elections for the National Assembly were held in December 1991. We use the word 'free' here with caution. For the first time the KMT found itself in competition with a legal political opposition, the Democratic Progressive Party (DPP)[2], raising the possibility of the future transfer of power. The DPP had moved from Hallin's 'sphere of unacceptable controversy' to the 'sphere of legitimate controversy' (see Chapter 2) where its personalities and platform acquired a new visibility within the mainstream media. The government did allow free campaigning via television, but only between 9:05 and 9:35 pm (*China Times,* 4 December 1991). Moreover, each party had to submit beforehand its campaign tapes for scrutiny by the Central Election Commission to ensure each party 'adhered to the terms of the ROC'; all references to an independent Taiwan were deleted (Chou & Myers, 1998). The reaction to the broadcasts was muted:

Many people did not watch the television campaign, and some of those who did misunderstood which party stood for what. A telephone survey found that only 18 percent of those polled watched the program; of those polled, about two–thirds viewed the political advertising from beginning to end. Half the households reported that they did not believe such political information would influence how they voted. More than half the voters did not know what the election was about. Nearly 60 percent of those polled reported that they did not understand the various categories of electing candidates ... (Chou & Myers, 1998).

Democracy clearly had to travail a long and winding road before Chen Shui–bian's victory in the 2000 election provided the first signs of genuine consolidation, and indications that television campaigning had been embraced by candidates and voters alike.

The KMT's unsurprising 71.7 per cent victory[3] in the 1991 election appeared to give the party a new mandate, and suggested that the KMT could survive in a multi–party competitive democracy (though the party's vote–buying activities were a concern for international observers. See *Commons Daily*, 23 December, 1991). The elections for the Legislative Yuan were held twelve months later. Peter J. Moody (1995) has commented on these elections:

Everyone had known that these changes were inevitable, but most observers had not thought them possible before the mid–1990s. These elections perhaps mark the regime's attainment of full democracy. *They also ended any rationale for the Taipei regime to claim that it represented the whole of China* (emphasis added).

The domination of the Legislative Yuan and the National Assembly by delegates elected in 1947 was confined to the dustbin of history. Clearly this had implications for security within Taiwan. The political system built by the KMT and transferred to the island of Taiwan in 1949 had rested on the premise that the Republic of China would eventually re–take the mainland in a blaze of glory. As previous chapters have illustrated, this faith structured the way the party–government reacted to opposition within Taiwan, and justified the apparent permanence of ostensibly 'temporary' martial law provisions. Such reasoning passed away with the gerontocracy and the end of full diplomatic relations with the United States. Outdated world views would only hinder Taiwan's progress and offset the problems associated with international de–recognition.

Further reforms introduced by Lee included the direct election of the President and Vice–President, the provincial governor of Taiwan (a post abolished in 1998), and of the mayors of Taipei and Kaohsiung. Most significant for our discussion was the abolition of the Taiwan Garrison Command, raising hopes that the island's media would enjoy the freedom of speech it had long sought. This optimism was given a further boost with momentous changes to the constitution in 1992 following a lengthy battle over Article 100 (the so–called criminal code). This Article stated that 'if any person behaves as if he or she *intends* to destroy the national polity, steal or take over national property, use illegal means to change the nation's constitution, or actually carries out these intentions, then that person has committed a crime of domestic criminal violence.' (Chao & Myers, 1998) comment that the Garrison Command 'frequently invoked Article 100 to charge critics of the regime with endangering the nation's security ...' Critics, however, noted that the Article 'seriously invades the freedom of thought and speech of another person, which are guaranteed by the constitution'. Chen Shui–bian, for example, then only a Legislator, argued that 'All nonviolent political action falls within the scope of freedom of speech and should be protected by the constitution' (Chao &Myers, 1998). Article 100 was finally changed (though not abolished as many DPP Legislators had hoped) in 1992. The revised version clearly defined what it called 'domestic upheaval', and said: 'If there is no act of violence and no threatening behaviour, there will be no punishment' (Chao & Myers, 1998). The amendment to Article 100 was a landmark occasion in Taiwan's political and social transition, for it delineated the onset of a new era, one that would be devoid of arbitrary 'White Terror' tactics of power.

Of course open and direct elections also implied the ROC enjoyed a *de facto*, if not *de jure* sovereignty that only extended over Taiwan and its outlying islands. Long before Lee made his 'state–to–state' remarks on German radio in 1999, the President had formally ended the state of war with the PRC in the early 1990s. Together with free elections, this made the Chinese uneasy who, since then, have considered such political moves the precursor of a declaration of independence. On 23 March 1996, the people of Taiwan were given the opportunity for the first time in their history to participate in democratic elections for their President and Vice-President, elections that 'coincided' with Chinese missile tests off Taiwan's coast. If the tests were designed to intimidate Taiwan and weaken President Lee's authority at the polls, they backfired. Instead voters were more determined than ever to stand up to Beijing and thus elected Lee with a stunning 54 per cent of the vote. Perhaps the secretary–general of the KMT was not joking when he described China's President Jiang Zemin as the party's most valuable campaign manager.[4]

This chapter considers first the process of Taiwan's liberalisation. The media were part of the process, but only a small part. As previous discussions have suggested, Taiwan's democratisation was essentially elite–driven with opposition pressure acting as a further influence. The media *serve* democratisation, but are unable to drive the political agenda. The underground media had wide appeal, but were not considered a serious challenge. Hence the opposition media were tolerated as long as they did not try to organise a political movement against the government. The political organisations and personalities *using* these media as a front for their activity provoked the government to respond in often oppressive ways.

This discussion of liberalisation will be succeeded by an investigation of how well Taiwan's media have served and furthered the two remaining criteria of democratic consolidation, namely participation and competition. While the government's many efforts to create a more liberal media environment in Taiwan are certainly commendable, ownership patterns that distort the political agenda still restrict participation and political competition. These focus on, and thereby promote, the KMT party of government. John Keane (1991) has identified the need for the development of a 'plurality of non–state media' in democracies 'which both function as permanent thorns in the side of political power ... and serve as the primary means of communication for citizens situated within a pluralistic society'.

In Taiwan the task of satisfying Keane has been bestowed upon the so–called new media. TTV, CTV and CTS are still in no position to 'act as permanent thorns in the side of political power' due to prevailing patterns of ownership and influence. For example, just prior to the election for the Legislative Yuan in 1992, the KMT's Department of Cultural Affairs (DCA) stood accused of demanding that these stations refrain from broadcasting anything relating to the DPP's platform, or providing information about that party's candidates. These accusations were fiercely contested by the DCA which claimed that given the government's long involvement in the three television stations, the KMT no longer needs to issue formal instructions. Instead, there is a tacit understanding that the networks will act as their own censor. Such an environment does not provide for the development of an independent and objective Fourth Estate that is obliged to be critical of the government when necessary. Nor does it allow for the expression of a plurality of opinion. Hence the new media – and cable in particular – are providing the people of Taiwan with alternative information, opinion and, via the popularity of call–in programmes, greater opportunities to participate in the political process (though, as on TVBS's call–in programmes viewers are restricted to voicing their opinions in the last five minutes of the programme. This is hardly 'political participation'). In turn this will have long–term benefits for the consolidation of democracy.

The Media and Liberalisation: The 'New Media'

The process of democratisation in Taiwan has been far from linear. The boundaries between liberalisation and political reform were often blurred and difficult to identify. Nevertheless, it is clear that reform of the media environment proceeded as part of the movement towards full liberalisation that started in 1987, even though it was slow and protracted. Restrictions on the publication of daily newspapers were not lifted until January 1988 (at which time there were just 31 legal newspapers published.[5] By August 1999, this figure had risen to 393. Government Information Office, 1999); areas of the electronic media were liberalised only after political reform – receiving and transmitting cable television broadcasts remained illegal until 1993 (some twenty–four years after cable had first arrived on the island), while call–in radio stations were only legalised in 1994, though underground radios continue to broadcast due to the high costs of entry to the market; the Publication Laws that controlled the press via strict licensing regulations were not abolished until 1999 upon the recommendation of the GIO. At the time of writing (the end of 1999), the KMT still enjoys considerable influence over TTV, CTV and CTS, as well as the majority of radio networks.[6] Prior to 1993, there were only 33 legal radio broadcasting stations in Taiwan. By October 1999, the number increased to 118, with another 27 under construction. The GIO explains this rapid and welcome expansion with reference to the release in mid–1999 of 72 frequencies that were previously reserved for the needs of the military and the telecommunications industry (*Taiwan's Media in the Democratic Era*, 1999).

It is clear that political liberalisation stimulated a quick response by Taiwan's media. The media were swept along by the developing political climate and the popular mood for greater and quicker change, and many within the industry wondered why the media could not be liberated immediately with the lifting of martial law. A general movement was created that liberalised the media before the appropriate legislation was in place. In other words, the media liberalised themselves, rather than waiting to be liberalised by the government's legal machinery. Such impulses also captured the popular imagination, and the slow liberalisation of the media became itself a prominent political issue. Cable television channels and call–in radio stations proliferated between 1987 and 1993, even though neither were legal at that time. Not only did such 'new' media suggest that people expected and demanded greater diversity in ownership and content – giving more choice in both – but their creation and popularity were viewed as an organised and deliberate response to the unhurried change in the mainstream media. Often popular activities directed against the bias of the electronic mainstream media – and the three national television stations in particular – had been used as a method of mobilising opposition against the government. The DPP had been especially active in this regard, and many of its members have been involved in the scholarly debate about the future of Taiwan's media. This means that media issues themselves had a tendency to become highly politicised. Media issues have frequently developed into *political* issues, and the 'three outs' – getting political parties, the government, and the military out of the three network TV stations – became a central demand of the opposition movement. The following provides a clear idea of the some of the more significant events in the chronology (after Fang, 1995; also Cheng *et.al.* 1993):

30 November 1989   The DPP's candidate for Taipei county mayor, Yu Ching, launched the illegal 'Democratic Progressive TV Station'.

1 March 1990   The 'Voice of Democracy' pirate radio station was organised by the comedian and radio presenter, Wu Le-tien. Its equipment was confiscated by the GIO on 31 March 1990.

23 September 1990   The union for 21 local branches of the 'Democratic Progressive TV Station' was established, organising a movement to 'liberate' television.

25 October 1990   The 'Taiwanese Democratic TV Station' began transmitting.

28 February 1991   On the anniversary of 2–28, the DPP published its plan to 'liberate' television.

1 October 1991   Wu Le–tien established the 'Voice of Taiwan' radio station.

10 January 1992 | The 'Democratic Progressive TV Union' (DPU) jammed the frequencies on which CTS broadcast its news programmes.

1 February 1992 | Part of the DPU's equipment was confiscated by the GIO.

15 February 1992 | The DPU published a half–page advertisement in *Liberty Times, The Independent Morning Post*, and *The Independent Evening Post* that accused the government of having monopolised radio and television frequencies.

Underground radio fared little better (after Fang, 1995 & 1998):

1 March 1990 | The DPP's Chang Chun–hung illegally established the Voice of Democracy radio station in Taipei. Between March and October, branches were established in Kaohsiung, Pingtung, and Taipei county.

November 1993 | The Voice of Taiwan was established by Hsu Jung–chi.

22 February 1994 | The Voice of Taiwan, an underground radio station, appealed to taxi drivers to gather in front of the Ministry of Finance to protest against high insurance premiums. In March, talk–radio host, Hsu Jung–chi, and others were prosecuted by the Taipei Judicial Office and jailed for eight months . Hsu was charged under a law banning illegal public gatherings. 'Freedom of speech is not a crime. This is political repression,' he shouted as police dragged him away after the sentence was passed.

21 April 1994 | Again, the Voice of Taiwan mobilised hundreds of taxies to surround the KMT Central Office. The Taipei Judicial Office confiscated equipment used by the Voice of Taiwan and other radio stations on the grounds that they encouraged criminal activity.

Meanwhile, the New Voice of Formosa, an underground radio station, began broadcasting in Hakka for one hour per day.

30 July 1994   By July, the number of underground stations island–wide had multiplied to fourteen. The GIO confiscated their equipment, claiming that they were breaking the law in broadcasting. The DPP held a press conference to voice their protest. The Taipei city government disagreed with the GIO's action, and the county magistrate announced that the county police force would not co–operate with the GIO. Legislators proposed opening up channels and then legalise underground radio.

1–3 August 1994   The GIO's actions led to violence. The government announced that the rioters would be prosecuted, and illegal stations would continue to be closed down. The DPP responded by affirming that people had the right to resist such action, but agreed violence should be avoided. Both the DPP and the New Party held the KMT's monopoly on channels as the root of the problem.

31 August 1994   Equipment used by the Voice of Taiwan and the Voice of the Public was confiscated.

22–25 December 1994   The number of underground stations reached fifty. The Taiwan Nation radio station was closed down.

3 January 1995   The Formosa New Voice radio station was closed down. The mayor of Taipei, the DPP's Chen Shui-bian, suggested legalising underground stations.

6 January 1995   Equipment used by the Formosa New Voice and New Thinking radio stations was confiscated The DPP again called for the opening up of channels.

10 January 1995   The Formosa New Voice radio station mobilised 1500 listeners to gather at the Legislative Yuan in

Taipei and protest against the neglect of Hakka culture.

11 January 1995   The New Thinking and Formosa New Voice stations were again raided by the GIO.

12 January 1995   Six stations in Kaohsiung were closed down by the GIO.

14 January 1995   New Thinking was again raided by the GIO. The Big Taipei radio station was also targeted, even though it had not yet started broadcasting.

16 January 1995   The GIO closed eight stations, including Taiwan Nation, Voice of Truth, and Sweet Potato.

21 January 1995   The Chiayi branch of the Voice of Taiwan and the Kaohsiung branch of Sweet Potato were closed by the GIO. Two others were also targeted. Two DPP legislators (one of whom now owns the Formosa Television Corporation) tried to negotiate with the GIO in Kaohsiung, but failed.

23 January 1995   Hsu Jung-chi, host of the Voice of Taiwan, began a hunger strike in Washington DC to protest against the GIO's actions.

6 February 1995   Underground stations located in Taipei, Taichung, Chiayi, Taichung, and Kaohsiung organised a one hour joint broadcast as a protest.

These chronologies clearly reveal that the opposition were still prepared to organise and use illegal media channels even after many of their political demands were met. More importantly perhaps, it also indicates that the government still felt that these media presented a serious threat to its power and chose to confiscate vital broadcasting equipment. The people wanted to exercise their new–found political rights of participation and demanded greater competition within the media environment that might assist the creation of a truly plural society. The government did not wish to rush the process. Yet we must note the persistence of opposition radio stations in particular. Many had their equipment confiscated one day, only to be broadcasting again the next. Their demands to be heard could not be suppressed. The title of these radio stations provide an indication of their political orientation: the Formosan New Voice, for example, and the Voice of Taiwan (rather than the Republic of China), both stations that were very popular among taxi drivers (the traditional base of support for the DPP) and were able to mobilise political activities. This 'incitement', sometimes encouraging the expression of a distinctly Taiwanese voice, worried the government and explains their reaction.

So why did the government decide to legalise such media? In the case of cable television, it had little choice. As Sheila Chin has noted, cable television in Taiwan 'originated from regular Common Antennas Television (CATV) systems and the activities of "Fourth Channels" set up by cable television pirates and political opposition' (Sreberny–Mohammadi, 1997). The term, the 'Fourth Channel' was used by the public in Taiwan to refer to its status as an illegal addition to the three official stations. Unlicensed stations had existed since 1969, but had few viewers due mainly to the low quality of programming offered. The launch of AsiaSat 1 in April 1990 changed all that. Now programmes could be delivered (illegally) by satellite and the illegally redistributed by cable operators, making it much easier for audiences to receive a variety of alternative programmes. Their quality was still questionable, and one should resist the temptation to believe that the 'Fourth Channel' was committed only to providing a voice for opposition politics: 'Its popularity stemmed from its ability to broadcast material unavailable on free–to–air stations, such as Japanese TV series, professional wrestling, and pornography' – hardly a heady mix of programmes that would change the world![7]

In 1985, the GIO had already started to research the cable environment, and in 1989 began work on a draft law to regulate an over–chaotic illegal market. This was prompted by pressure from American television stations who protested the redistribution of their programming by illegal cable stations without payment or permission. By 1991, cable television served only 40,000 households (Sreberny–Mohammadi, 1997). Just prior to the passage of the Cable TV Law in 1993, cable had already penetrated almost half of Taiwan's households. The Legislative Yuan, therefore, only legalised an already wide–spread and extremely popular phenomenon. By 1995, cable television accounted for 60 - 70 per cent of the market (23 per cent in Hong Kong, 8 per cent in Japan, *Free China Review*, February 1996); by 1999, the market penetration had increased to 80 per cent, the highest in the Asia–Pacific region (*Taiwan's Media in the Democratic Era*).

Underground radio has never been legalised in the true sense of the word. Instead, the government has relaxed regulations that governed the creation of new community–based radio stations and invited applications for licenses to operate on newly opened frequencies. In August 1996, the New Telecommunications Law was passed that reaffirmed underground radio stations would continue to be prosecuted and their operators fined or jailed. This has not deterred the pirates of the airwaves: by the end of 1997, there were an estimated 80 to 90 underground radio stations that defied the government.

Formosa Hakka Radio is Taiwan's first Hakka radio station, and is an instructive example of a station that made the transfer from being an illegal underground operation to a legal and very successful broadcasting company that services a minority audience.[8] In 1993, there were no stations in Taipei, legal or otherwise, that broadcast in Hakka. One survey carried out in 1995 discovered that less than 1.5 per cent of Taiwan's radio output was in Hakka, even though 12 per cent of the population spoke that language. The media had been inhibited by the Regulatory Guidelines for Broadcast Radio and Television Programming which declared that programming in minority languages could not account for more than 55 per cent of the total output. In 1976, further regulations required AM stations to broadcast a minimum of 50 per cent Mandarin programming, and FM stations a minimum of 70 per cent. The restrictions were revised by the Legislative Yuan in 1993, and broadcasts in minority languages were now legally and politically guaranteed (see Chapter 1). The GIO finally approved Formosa Hakka Radio's application for a license in July 1996, though the station then found itself subject to a new ostensibly non–political pressure: how to raise NT$30 million in funding in just six months. The temptation to define such legal stipulations as purely market oriented and driven by considerations other than the government's desire to control the creation of potentially dangerous stations, is too difficult to resist. Fund–raising exceeded all expectations and the station received far more donations than were required. There are many anecdotes to support the effect that Formosa Hakka Radio has had. Some report a renaissance of 'Hakka consciousness':

Liu Mei–chih, a teacher at Chungli's Hsinchieh Primary School, became a regular and enthusiastic listener when she became aware of the existence of Formosa Hakka Radio. She and her husband began speaking Hakka in their home and teaching the language to their children. Over the course of two years, the children have learned some everyday conversation, and their eldest daughter even founded a Hakka club at her high school.[9]

Minority–language radio benefited from the release of 72 frequencies in mid–1999 that were previously reserved for the needs of the military and the telecommunications industry. 42 of these frequencies were for regional stations and 30 for community stations. Seven were allocated to the National Education Radio, four for aboriginal programming, and five for Hakka. Government–owned radio stations have responded to the re–assertion of Taiwan's multi–ethnic identity by providing an ever increasing amount of programming in regional dialects. The Broadcasting Corporation of China (BCC) and the Central Broadcasting System (CBS) offer programmes in Southern Fukienese, while the Cheng Sheng Broadcasting Corporation (CSBC) broadcast in Mandarin, Southern Fukienese and Hakka. CSBC tailors its programming for Taiwan's agricultural, fishing and labour communities, thus reinforcing the idea that the media must take into account the growing power of civil society (see Chapter 4).

Markets and the Consolidation of Democracy

Cable television has been increasingly important in strengthening the growth of Taiwan's civil society. By encouraging pluralism within the media environment the new media promote individual freedom of choice. Audiences are less dependent on official sources or sources of information that are centred on Taipei. They potentially serve more specialist audiences, and should promote more popular control over the media (McQuail, 1987). Because of the local flavour of cable programming, due primarily to the limited range of frequencies allocated to broadcasters, programmes can be tailored to accommodate the diversity of Taiwan's modern society. As such, cable programming constitutes a critical part of what Dahlgren (1995) has called the 'advocacy domain', and his views are worth quoting at length for their normative implications:

> This advocacy domain would be the setting for all citizens who wish to pursue special interests, and generate group–based cultural and political interpretations of society. Ideally, marginalized and oppressed groups would be assisted with financial and technical means to enable their participation in the advocacy domain. The advocacy domain would serve partly as alternative and oppositional public spheres for different groups ... allowing them not only to air and shape their own views, but also to develop their group identities. This domain would also function as an organized source, providing dialogic, contesting voices for the common domain. *The net result would be ... multiperspective journalism, which would help*

counter the prevailing understanding that there is only one version of what constitutes truth or reality and only one way to talk about it [emphasis added].

We remain cautious and argue that the new media should not be a substitute for national broadcasting systems because 'narrowcasting' creates its own problems.   This is a term used to refer to the way programmes target and appeal to specific audiences, usually geographic or demographic. In Taiwan, narrowcasting certainly provides a substitute to the Taipei–dominated mainstream media, and because of the local nature of such programming, it offers the possibility that a stronger social relationship between the source and audience might develop. However, narrowcasting only further divides the audience, since they will seek out those programmes that correspond to their own political orientation, and thus insulate them from alternatives. As James Robinson (1996) has noted, 'cable news coverage and talk shows did not make for notably more objective comment. Instead, they promoted greater competition in biased reporting'.   Many stations promoted the policies and personalities associated with the opposition parties, and justified such bias by explaining that they were simply remedying an already disagreeable situation; bias for the opposition is warranted, because it balances the bias of the mainstream media towards the KMT government.[10]

The creation of a new media environment that will take its rightful place in a democratic Taiwan requires more than the opening up of a plurality of channels that cater for minority interests.   To avoid the limitations of narrowcasting and secure the consolidation of democracy, further liberalisation of the existing mainstream television system is crucial. The current danger is that the legalisation of the new media has softened the demand for further liberalisation of the mainstream television channels. Neither has Taiwan's cable television industry been in a position to resist the concentration of ownership that characterises other forms of media. Immediately after legalisation, the KMT ensured that it would have as big a stake as possible in the new television market, and mobilised its legislators to amend the Cable and Television Law to allow political parties to invest in the cable industry. While rapid advances in communications technology appear to encourage pluralism, we must also be mindful that the diversity in management of the new media are subject to myriad political and legal restrictions that can often serve as a form of indirect form of central control and influence.

Moreover, the principles of market capitalism within the cable and satellite industry create the problems that are associated with commercialism. A national survey revealed in 1995 that cable channels broadcast more entertainment shows than the three national television stations in order to attract the largest possible advertising revenues (Hwang, 1996). Cable operators not only compete among themselves, but also with the satellite industry and the five networks (the old three plus Formosa Television and the Public Television System). The result of such fierce competition is that the quality and content of many locally produced entertainment and niche market programmes on the cable channels suffer. High production costs and market competition inhibit the diversity that the cable system was meant to provide; they are legally required to produce a fixed quota of locally–produced programmes – 20 per cent in 1993, rising to 25 per cent in 1996 (Fang, 1995) – but they often meet this by creating low–quality productions or by simply copying the formats of successful programmes on other channels. Quality after all relies on the possession of the requisite skills, equipment (and there is still a tendency towards uneven distribution of these throughout society) and a strong market incentive. There are signs that Taiwan's market cannot sustain a growing cable industry: the number of cable companies island–wide shrank from 600 in the early 1990s to a mere 70 at the end of the decade (*Taipei Times*, 7 January 2000).

Some have also identified problems associated with the non–dialogical character of call–in programmes and talk–radio, and have suggested that contrary to opinion they contribute little to popular participation (Thompson, 1993). Those who have studied the phenomenon in the United States have had reason to be cynical about its use and value. Talk–radio is closely associated with the growing dissatisfaction with politicians and politics in general across the United States, and with what has been described as a national obsession with 'rant and rave time' (Diamond & Silverman, 1995). Edwin Diamond and Robert A. Silverman have concluded that 'the best thing that can be said about talk radio may be that it provides an outlet for venting some of the anger endemic in America,' and their cynicism underscores their lack of confidence in the medium's democratic potential:

> In the wired nation, the call–in programmes and the talk–show hosts present themselves as facilitators of the "power of the people". In grandiose fashion – the normal mode of such discourse – their shows are described as "democracy in action". The existence of new outlets for the exchange of political beliefs and the expression of self–interest *sounds* like a positive, bracing development; it can be taken as self–evident that public policy counts. In practice, the talk–show culture too often exchanges only the

mutual ignorance of listeners and hosts who share mainly a taste for ranting and raving.

It is difficult to be this sceptical of Asia's experience with call–in programmes.   Their role in providing greater opportunities for political participation has provoked one scholar to observe that 'the prevalence or otherwise of talk radio serves as a crude barometer of the degree of political freedom countries enjoy' (Elegant, 1996).   In Thailand, for example, talk–radio and television became popular when people began to call the media to sound off about the 1992 demonstrations, despite the government and military retaining a tight grip over the media (Elegant, 1996).   Other examples could be culled from Indonesia, Malaysia and Singapore with varying degrees of openness and extremes.   In Taiwan, the medium's role and influence suggest that systems in transition value the opportunity to 'rant and rave' as symbolic of their newly discovered freedom of speech: 'Listeners are eager to express their views about national development and question over the air officials who appear at the studios to answer questions' (*Republic of China Yearbook, 1996*).   Commenting on the role of call–in programmes during the 1994 elections, Hu Fo said that 'many people felt much more involved in the elections' (*Free China Review*, February 1995).   This is an encouraging sign that the so–called new media are gradually opening spaces for political debate, and are thus fostering the further consolidation of Taiwan's democratic culture.   Indeed the government itself has recognised the contribution that call–in programmes can make to democracy.   In October 1993, the national Broadcasting Corporation of China established a 'Minister's Hotline' that allowed government officials to be scrutinised by the public.   As a national event, this was an exception; most call–in shows are broadcast on those radio stations that form part of the new media.   It is true that these do experience many of the same problems as cable television in terms of narrowcasting, and in heightening popular expectations of what can be achieved. Moreover, the national radio spectrum is still dominated by the KMT.

However, it cannot be denied that through a multiplicity of channels, an increasingly informed citizenry are given wider opportunities to participate and compete in the political process. The role of the new media in the consolidation of democracy is much more difficult to determine. For example the internet should have provided the greatest opportunity for empowerment of previously marginalised members of society. Thus 'ethnic minorities, gay/lesbians and political or artistic dissidents, now have a venue of expression that has traditionally been closed to them'.[11]   But having a discussion forum is radically different from empowerment which suggests *participation in the political process*. The creation of 'niche' websites – internet discussion groups that cater for specialised interests and tastes – merely perpetuates the problems of 'narrowcasting' found in other areas of the media. Specialised internet sites rarely usually preach beyond the already converted; such websites may in fact be a method of *containing* the unwanted elements in society rather than empowering them. The new media enjoy an enviable position to encourage the growth of civil society, but until Taiwan's media environment is reformed to allow the mainstream media to perform the functions expected by democracy, the new media will only maintain the divisive and adversarial political culture:

> Through these [call–in] shows the voters can air their opinions to their heart's content – people are able to pass judgement on political figures and even yell at them. It is through this medium that a model of electronic democracy is taking shape' (Chen Chun-hung, *Taipei Times*, 13 December 1999).

Nevertheless, 'the speed and efficiency of the electronic media may have created more chances to express opinions but they do not guarantee the public a better understanding of the issues' (*ibid.*). Call–in programmes are most popular during elections, though callers rarely get the opportunity to express more than their personal preference of candidate.

Consolidation

The achievements of democratisation are impressive: Consolidation is much more difficult to achieve. This calls for political rights and freedoms to be established as customary practices in the public psyche and within government institutions. It also demands checks against backsliding, so that the consummation of democracy is preserved (Huntington, 1991). Consolidation refers to 'the embedding of democratic procedures into the infrastructure as a whole so that the system is secure and is generally seen as the appropriate way of organising political life' (Gill, 2000). The responsibility for educating and informing the people about how democracy can and should work falls to the media (a liberal view, explored by Huntington & Nelson, 1976). The media can also teach by example; by encouraging debate on public issues, scrutinising the activities of all political parties, and engaging with individual politicians on the issues of the day, the media open up a public forum that nourishes the a popular understanding of democratic practice. Nie & Verba (1975) referred to this as the creation of 'a syndrome of supportive civic attitudes'.

Media liberalisation allowed the government to publicise and thus legitimise its political transformation. It increased popular awareness and understanding of the changing political agenda, while at the same time granting the opposition a legal voice. The media are today certainly more critical of the government than at any time in the past. The media now feel a responsibility to hold the political process to account. In the second half of 1999, for example, the repercussions of the earthquake continued to reverberate through the media long after the tremors had eased. The media were central in questioning the performance of the government in responding to the problems caused by the earthquake: re–housing, welfare, unemployment, the problems faced by the aboriginal tribes that lost everything at the epicentre, the need to investigate who was responsible for the inferior construction of many homes and schools (raising questions of political corruption that damaged the KMT in particular). Other problems were equally intractable, such as the public outcry over the National Assembly's decision in September 1999 to extend its own life. The media were not prepared to let these issues just disappear. In other words, the media have contributed more to the *consolidation* of democracy in Taiwan than to democratisation itself.

Competitive direct elections with a high level of participation are considered to be one of the principle criteria of democratic consolidation. (This contests the narrow Schumpeterian idea of elections as the cornerstone of a minimalist or procedural democracy.[12]) Elections are therefore the flash points in the political calendar when a liberalised media should come into its own:

> The media must inform people about the different parties and candidates and help them to choose from among them. They should also be the watchdogs, exposing instances of electoral malpractice. At the same time they must help to keep up the pressure for change (Randall, 1993).

The media are central to participatory democracies, implying their encouragement of debate, deliberation, and active popular involvement (Robinson & White, eds. 1998).

However, the mainstream media remain dominated by images of KMT candidates (magnifying the importance of incumbency), and are therefore unable to fully and freely inform the electorate about alternative candidates and platforms. In addition, the often vicious and usually uncorroborated personal attacks on candidates suggest that Taiwan's political culture has yet to grasp the existence of the fine line between freedom of speech and the responsibilities that must accompany the acceptance of electoral democracy (Rawnsley, 1997).

The post–democratisation era has witnessed a social and political reassertion of the Taiwanese identity. Lee Teng–hui's attendance at a remembrance ceremony for the victims of 2–28 indicated that history would no longer be whitewashed. There has also been a remarkable renaissance in Taiwanese art and historical studies, all focused on the quest to renew acquaintance with the Taiwanese, ie. non–mainland identity. Among the younger generation in particular, 'identification with a China that includes the mainland was becoming an abstract notion and their primary concern was their own welfare on the island' (quoted in Klintworth, 1995).

A major player in this new media and political environment is a fourth national television channel. On 28 January 1994, the GIO announced the release of a new island–wide commercial television channel to be based in Kaohsiung, Taiwan's biggest city in the south (*Min Sheng Pao*, 29 January 1994). Three groups vied for control, suggesting that competition was taking hold and would fuse politics, society and business. The first group was 'Asian Pacific Television', organised by the Chen Tien-mao family that enjoyed close strong personal ties with the KMT. The second proposal was drafted by 'People's United Television' (PUTV), headed by four prominent DPP politicians, Yu–Chen Yueh–ying, Tien Tsai–ting, Chang Chun–hung, and Tsai Tung–jung. The third was 'Harvest Television', organised by a collection of celebrities with wide experience of producing television programmes (*Central Daily News*, 24 August 1994). Asian Pacific Television submitted the strongest proposal and enjoyed the strongest financial foundation. Thus commentators were shocked when the GIO granted the licence to the DPP's PUTV in June 1995 (*Central Daily News*, 18 June 1995). After two years of meticulous preparation, PUTV renamed itself Formosa Television Corporation (FTC) with DPP politician, Tsai Tung–jung, at its head. FTC began transmitting island–wide in June 1997 from Kaohsiung. (*Free China Journal*, 20 June 1997). The creation of FTC was a landmark event in the media–politics interface. It broke the KMT's hold over mainstream television, and addressed previously taboo subjects. One of its most popular and innovative productions has been a drama serial set during the 28 February uprising. FTC is located in Kaohsiung, thus drawing attention from Taipei as the centre of activity in Taiwan – viewers now know that news happens outside the capital city! FTC also guarantees a large number of programmes in Taiwanese and is thus seen as promoting media diversity and competition. The Director of

FTC's News Department, Hu Yuan–hui, said in June 1998 that he hoped his station could become 'an opposition television station, rather than a television station of the opposition party' (*The Journalist*, 21–27 June 1998).   The pressing question is whether FTC will be an exclusively Taiwanese station, and thus perpetuate the primary division of identity within Taiwan, or whether it will provide equal resources and access for other minority language programming, and so provide a real alternative to the Mandarin–dominated KMT networks.[13]   Is the FTC's claim to be 'The People's Television' justified?   The results so far have not been encouraging.   The station is blatantly biased towards the DPP, and professional journalists working for the station feel they have an 'implicit responsibility' to provide more coverage of DPP politics than the other parties.[14]   One of the major problems that journalists face is that they are viewed as mouthpieces of the DPP both by other parties and *by the DPP itself*.   During the 1998 election for mayor of Taipei, journalists felt that they had been used by incumbent Chen Shui–bian to spread his propaganda and attack his opponents.   One must therefore concede that while FTC does encourage pluralism in the media, the problem of bias remains.   This is suggested also by the fact that one third of its managerial positions are filled by DPP members and politicians.   Moreover, while its decision– making nerve centre remains in Kaohsiung, programming (especially news) has shifted to Taipei.   FTC is certainly considered to be a threat even in the age of media liberation.   Several journalists have expressed concern that their telephone conversations with their sources had been monitored by the government's security agencies.

These problems are increasingly circumscribed by an active and vocal cable and talk–radio broadcasting industry. These provide opposition candidates an opportunity to target their political propaganda for specific audiences and thus appeal to the voters most sympathetic to their platform. Their value to the creation of a civil society in Taiwan is unquestionable. In addition, the media have been central in exposing electoral malpractice and corruption, and in stimulating the movement against such behaviour:

> The idea of government ... is everywhere yielding to a broader sense of governance as people, non–government agencies, corporate and transnational bodies, and civil society generally come into their own. Deregulation has given individuals and communities far greater freedom of action. This perhaps places freedom of expression and of information in a new context as the State, from being the master–controller and regulator is more nearly becoming a player, although still perhaps more equal than others in a cybernetic environment (Verghese, 1996).

The opportunities that are presented by political liberalisation are tempered by other factors, most notably market forces, which are more or less beyond the control of any one individual or group; and these forces play a role of comparable power to political restrictions. Capitalism is uncontested ideologically (Falk, 1995). After all, political involvement in the media is a recognised enemy. The political environment is structured in such a way that interference can be resisted by institutionalised checks and balances, and by the emergence of strong forces of opposition. The effects of commercialism are more subversive and sinister since they legitimately erode the quality of programming via reference to such notions as 'free market forces' and 'value for money'. The market is not a panacea to the failures of state management of the media. Markets substitute the free flow of information for economic concentration, financial barriers to entering the market, and the pressures of advertising. The market is as antithetical as the intrusive state to the promotion of an informed citizenry that engages in reasoned public debate. For example, the print media remain dominated by a small assortment of powerful corporate interests that own and control groups of newspapers. In 1993, the consortia owning the three most important newspapers in Taiwan – the *China Times*, the *United Daily News*[15] and the *Liberty Times* (*Tzuyou Shihpao*, a new title that entered the industry in the post–reform era and responsible for the English language *Taipei Times*) – commanded the market with a combined share of 45 per cent (Weng & Sun, 1994). Since the groups owning these three newspapers have close links with the KMT, the political significance of this market superiority can not be overlooked.[16]

Nevertheless, it cannot be denied that the print media now enjoy greater editorial independence despite the persistence of traditional ownership patterns. But the role of censor is now played by the market, rather than government. Fierce competition for advertising revenue and readers has forced the print media to converge on the middle ground. This is clearly illustrated by the short–life of the *Capital Morning Post* (*Shoudu Zaopao*) which was established and financed by Kang Ning–hsing whom we met in the last chapter as the founder of the *Taiwan Political Review*. *Capital Morning Post* was forced to close down not because it advocated the opinion of the DPP and discussed the issues of 'unacceptable controversy', but because it captured an unsustainable share of the market. At the beginning of 2000, the GIO told the *Taiwan Daily News* (*Taiwan Shin Wen*), a military–owned newspaper based in Kaohsiung, that it may have to be closed down if it did not make a profit. To turn its fortunes around, the paper would have to be downsized into a local paper, and 100–

200 of its staff laid off (*Taipei Times*, 31 January 2000). Even state–owned media are no longer immune to market forces.

Competition in the market, which forces the press to concentrate on attracting the largest number of readers by consolidating their position on the middle ground, has also moderated the radicalism of previously dissident print media; the principal political journals that survive are either sponsored by big patrons who have the financial resources to support such ventures, or are small collections of articles by politically active intellectuals and require little financial assistance.[17] They are unable to compete with the finance of the major league players that have invested considerable sums in: upgrading their technology; responding to the changing tastes of readers at a moment's notice; recruitment of the brightest and the best; a four–fold increase in the number of pages published; and the introduction of evening newspapers (Yen, 1998).

Conclusions

Taiwan's recent experiences of political transition suggest a positive correlation between the promotion of free and diverse media and the level of systemic change. Liberalisation of the media is definitely a requisite for democratisation but, as happened in Taiwan, it may either precede or follow the introduction of more tangible political reform and thus give the process a much sharper focus.

Democracies are defined by the level of popular participation and competition allowed, and are therefore given form by a plurality of free and open media. Occupying a central position within democratic societies, the media act as mirrors of ideas and the catalyst for serious public debate. As many views and opinions as possible are discussed in order that individual citizens might make a full and worthwhile contribution to the political process. As Taiwan continues on the path towards full democracy the role of the media will undoubtedly increase; an efficient, independent and diverse media system is crucial for the successful consolidation of democratic procedure, and to protect the system against the possibility of decay. The new media do allow for the expression of views that are absent in the mainstream, but we would argue that until the mainstream itself is liberated to accommodate such opinion, the process of consolidation is in danger. As Randall (1993) has observed, 'If the media are to make their full contribution to democracy, there needs to be democracy *within* the media, dispersal of control over and access to the media to the whole range of local communities, minority groups and so on'. Some state regulation is advisable; a completely commercialised media only devalues their role as agents of political reconstruction and education. A concentration of private ownership can be just as dangerous as a state/party monopoly, while market competition focuses attention on seeking profit and audiences, rather than on the quality of output. The scale of government–manipulation of the cable industry has only recently surfaced. This is due primarily to the close business connections between members of the KMT and the business community. Some legislators have admitted that they or their colleagues have interfered in regulating the industry for their own financial benefit. In turn, several large cable operators have avoided investigation or regulation through their connections to the political system (*Taipei Times*, 3 February 2000). The two big players in the market are Rebar Corporation's Eastern Multimedia and United Communications. Together they control an estimated 80 per cent of the cable market. Eastern Multimedia is headed by Wang Ling–lin, a KMT legislator and a member of the party's central standing committee; United Communications was established by Koo Chen–fu, a senior member of the KMT who also chairs the Straits Exchange Foundation. The company is now run by his son, Koo Chih-yun. Observers believe that in the past both companies have escaped prosecution for their anti–competition practices because of their political connections. Clearly the 'electronic democracy' is not as democratic as idealists would have us believe.[18]

Particularly close attention needs to be devoted to monitoring the output and impact of the Formosa Television Corporation, Taiwan's newest national television station that first aired in June 1997. This is a welcome development that will inevitably encourage further democratisation. It is Taiwan's first fully private network station, and is located in Kaohsiung in the south of the island. It guarantees a significant number of programmes in the Taiwanese language; it holds out the prospect for greater competition within the media *à la* Randall; and although it promises that its Board of Directors (primarily drawn from the ranks of the DPP) will not influence its coverage, it is highly probable that it will be seen as a force to counter the other network television stations *(Free China Journal*, 20 June 1997).

Perhaps one solution to the problems that currently challenge Taiwan's television system lies in the development of a public service broadcasting station, free from both commercial and political pressure, and that is ultimately accountable to the people. John Keane (1993) passionately described his ideal public service television system that should, he said:

facilitate a genuine commonwealth of forms of life, tastes and opinion to empower a plurality of citizens who are governed neither by despotic states nor by market forces. It should enable them to live democratically within the framework of multilayered constitutional states which are held accountable to their citizens, who work and consume, live and love, quarrel and compromise within independent, self–organizing civil societies which underpin and transcend the narrow boundaries of state institutions.

There is no reason why Taiwan could not support such a system provided it is responsive to indigenous requirements; variations of the ideal have been adopted in other countries, including the United States, Japan and Britain, and Taiwan has studied these models with interest (M. Rawnsley, 1997). Taiwan is certainly in need of a genuine national public television institution that will function as a Fourth Estate, and would go someway towards allowing the people themselves, rather than the politicians, to define the political agenda. Although we are not suggesting that such a station will necessarily cure all the problems facing modern Taiwan, it would at least provide an open forum in which all problems and possible remedies can be discussed, problems that perhaps both the political establishment and the mainstream media currently prefer to ignore.

However, until 2000 the successful consolidation of democracy – if by consolidation we mean the peaceful transfer of power from one democratically elected government to another (Huntington, 1991) – was challenged by forces that are more powerful than any of those so far discussed: The PRC continued to exert a considerable influence over the transition to democracy and the agenda that was followed by the media. This was clearly illustrated during the 1996 Presidential election. Issues that are bound up with Taiwan's relations with China – national identity, the level of the threat from Beijing – structured almost every layer of Taiwan's political life. In turn, these very important issues framed the methods and content of political discourse in Taiwan, and thus drove the media's agenda. In other words, the media will never be completely independent until the complex issue of identity is resolved.

Notes

1. For further information about the fight over the redistribution of power within the KMT see Long (1991), Chen (1992), Tsang (ed., 1993), Chen (1995), Moody (1995), Ferdinand (ed, 1996), and Dickson (1997).
2. The DPP was actually formed in 1986. This made it illegal, though Chiang Ching–kuo allowed it to exist.

3.   The DPP achieved an impressive 23.94 per cent of votes. The remaining votes were shared between the People's Alliance, the China Social Democratic Party, and the People's Nonpolitical Alliance (Chou & Myers, 1998).

4.   For assessments of this landmark election, see Chu (1996); Hsieh & Niou (1996); Rawnsley (1997); Copper (1999); Tsang & Tien (1999).

5.   Two KMT–owned newspapers were closed down and the military–owned *Taiwan Daily News* was sold to individual entrepreneurs.

6.   Since 1949 the KMT party–state justified its control over most of Taiwan's radio frequencies in the interests of 'national security' (Cheng, 1993). The KMT–controlled Broadcasting Corporation of China (BCC) owned 32 per cent of transmitters and 52 per cent of radio power. In January 1997, the KMT decided to sell part of CTV's stock in two stages, releasing 8 per cent of its holdings first, and then 11 per cent. The party's share then became 48 per cent. In April 1999, CTV became a limited company, selling its shares on the stock exchange.

7.   See 'Cable Cat's Cradle', *Free China Review* (February 1996).

8.   This discussion is based on 'Formosa Hakka Radio – Taiwan's Hakka Find Their Voice', at www.taiwaninfo.org/info/sinorama/en/1998/199812/712094e1.htm

9.   www.taiwaninfo.org/info/sinorama/en/1998/199812/712094e1.htm

10. This was suggested by several interviews conducted at the FTC organisation, September 1999.

11. We are grateful to Allen Chun for letting us see his paper, jointly authored with Luke Cheng, 'The Growth of Internet Communities in Taiwan and the Marginalization of the Public Sphere'. Both are of the Institute of Ethnology in Taiwan's Academia Sinica. We are not as optimistic about the internet as many technophiles. See Chapter 5 for the downside to the internet revolution, particularly the creation of a new 'underclass'.

12. Schumpeter (1976) did not consider democracy to be 'an end in itself', but rather a 'mere method that could be discussed rationally' because it is 'that institutional arrangement for arriving at political decisions in which individuals acquire power to decide by means of a competitive struggle for the people's vote'. Schumpeter's view of democracy has been refined to form what might be considered a modern form of procedural democracy whereby elite power is circulated and governments are held to account.

13. The FTC has already become mired in the political divisions that revolve around identity. It has been criticised, mainly by New Party sympathisers among the overseas Chinese communities who receive programmes via satellite. Complaints centre on its use of Taiwanese greetings; its use of the terms 'China' and 'Taiwan' instead of 'Chinese communists' and 'Republic of China'; and their coverage of the opposition activist Cheng Nan–jung who committed suicide as a form of political protest. However, FTC has also received fulsome praise from overseas Chinese (*The Journalist*, 3–9 May 1998).

14. The authors are grateful to staff of the FTC for agreeing to talk to us in Taipei in 1999.

15. However, the *United Daily News* lost 90,000 copies in circulation following a boycott campaign led by prominent members of the DPP.

16. Yet the *China Times* and the *United Daily News* are still unable to prevent their readership from falling in a period of greater media diversity and competition, and especially a greater dependence on television as a source of news and information. In contrast, the readership of the *Liberty Times* is rising. This can be explained by

the fact that its owners have corporate interests in a number of other profitable ventures, thus allowing the *Liberty Times* to develop and withstand the shock to Taiwan's press industry. It can also be explained with reference to the remarkable number of activities that are used to promote a newspaper, many of which are familiar to readers of the British tabloid press (television advertisements, the giving away of prize 'scratch' cards, offers tied to subscription and, of course, a low cover price, etc. Teng, 1997).

17.   The only exception in Taiwan is the weekly magazine, *Journalist* (*Xin Xinwen*). This is a wholly independent and therefore objective publication that engages in investigative journalism.

18.   However at the beginning of 2000, the Taipei city government did penalise four cable companies for failing to stop the broadcast of unlicensed channels. All four companies, run by Eastern Multimedia, were fined a total of NT$12 million (*Taipei Times*, 7 January 2000).

4 Public Television and Empowerment

'For more than a generation, the public service broadcasting model has been considered a pillar of parliamentary democracy'
– John Keane (1993).

'We had some difficulty in obtaining an operational definition from broadcasters'
– The Peacock Committee (1986) on public service broadcasting in Britain (Scannel, 1989).

Introduction

Previous chapters have chronicled the development of commercial television and alternative media in Taiwan, and their relationship to political transition and critical security have been assessed. The discussion has centred on the twin ideas of *political control* and *emancipation*. Thus the media were central to the execution of authority by the KMT government and the political mobilisation of an opposition denied any meaningful democratic rights. The core notions of emancipation are normative and utilise such terms as 'rights', 'justice' and 'equality'. The British sociologist, Anthony Giddens (1991) has contrasted this 'emancipatory politics' with 'life politics' that are concerned more with one's relationship to the political and social system in the local, national and global spheres following emancipation. As the discussion so far has detailed the political and social struggles that demanded and, thanks partly to far–sighted elites and timely external pressures eventually secured emancipation via liberalisation, we now turn our attention to how 'life politics' have been shaped by and played out in the media. To explore this we find that it is useful to analyse Taiwan's public television system that has been broadcasting across the island since the early 1980s. This service was under total government control for the first decade of its existence. But with the deepening political liberalisation towards the end of the 1980s, the plan to transform this service into an independent public television station suddenly emerged as a focus of public debate at the beginning of the 1990s. Such open discussion had allowed the Taiwanese population to express its will through collective activities and to exercise the nascent power of civil society.

Civil society here refers to 'a sphere of activity outside direct state control, in which the citizenry may organize to pursue their own interests and concerns in their own way ...' (Gill, 2000), provided that the groups in question are voluntary (and not necessarily exclusive. Membership can be overlapping. Gellner, 1995). Although independent of state control (Hall, 1995; Bobbio, 1989), Gill makes the qualification that the activity of civil society must be recognised as legitimate by the state. While the routine of the expanding election culture served to empower the people during the 1970s and 1980s, issues of immediate concern to citizens (certainly more pressing than the ubiquitous cross-Strait relations) such as the environment, pollution, unemployment, housing, problems in Taiwan's agricultural sector and fears about the nuclear industry – Taiwan's own 'life politics' agenda – all grabbed attention and were played out in the media. Shiau Chyuan–jenq (1999) traces the origin of an active civil society in Taiwan to the journal *China Tide* which supported those who suffered because of the government's commitment to a capitalistic mode of production. However, while the early 1980s saw a remarkable increase in the number of civil challenges to the state's economic management, civil society could only operate in Taiwan once the political system had been liberalised to allow such autonomous activity to flourish. Thus after 1986 there was a rapid increase in the number and variety of social movements that protested the government's administration in several key areas: consumer movements; the environment; opposition to the nuclear industry; economic interests (farmers, women, education); minorities and the disadvantaged; and human rights (Shiau, 1999). Yet the first indication of the rise of a genuine civil society in Taiwan that was able to launch an effective challenge to the state's managerial capacity was the legalisation of the Democratic Progressive Party; although Taiwan's democratisation was essentially elite driven, we must be mindful that the strength of the political opposition lay in the broad societal support it enjoyed. The opposition was thus able to claim legitimacy based on its representative function. Once the regime opened the political system to permit challenges to its rule, civil society became more active in shaping the contours of the transition. However, the election of DPP President, Chen Shui–bian has not finalised the transition of the party as a leading force within civil society to its incorporation into the state structure. Throughout his election campaign Chen maintained that, if elected, he would distance himself from the DPP: 'After I am inaugurated,' he said at a final rally on the eve of the election, 'I will step out of participation in all DPP activities and become a president who can look beyond party and ethnic lines' (*Taipei Times*, 18 March 2000). Hence many DPP members and supporters who defend the party's more traditional, some might say radical, platform have not been encouraged by Chen's moderate position on a number of issues. This is especially true in reference to cross-strait relations, where his critics within the party believe he has 'sold out' their commitment to Taiwan's independence.[1] All of this leads to the observation that the DPP remains part of civil society, detached from the state, even though Chen was elected President on a (moderate) DPP platform.

Yet while we can claim that the peaceful transition of power from the KMT has signalled the completion of the transition to democracy in Taiwan, we must be mindful that civil society movements that exist and function *outside* political parties are only just developing into vibrant organisations (as of April 2000 there were 3,435 'civic organisations' in Taiwan).[2] This is important for the consolidation of democracy. While the election of Chen as President in 2000 indicated the consolidation of *procedural* democracy (a procedural minimum)[3], it is important to encourage the growth and participation of autonomous groups of political actors that can reinforce society's democratic values, and that can balance the power of political elites.[4] At the same time we should note that the existence of civil society does not necessarily imply inevitable conflict with the state. In fact, civil society requires a state structure for protection and to ensure the basic social conditions in which such autonomous groups can function (Giner, 1995). In the same way that we have previously recognised the benefits of state organisation (see our Introduction to this volume), civil society is neither simply a threat *to* the state, nor is it threatened *by* the state (Gellner, 1995). Modern democracy presupposes their co–existence as each has a significant role to play in representing and mediating their members' interests through the political process.

As the vitality of civil society presumes the existence of a public sphere within which issues are discussed and pressed (Gill, 2000), the idea of a public television station, free from political interference gains prominence. Although problematic in its simplicity, we accept for the purpose of this discussion the succint definition of public service broadcasting provided by Nicholas Garnham (1997):

> The essence of public service broadcasting is the provision, to all citizens on equal terms and as an enabling condition of such citizenship, of a site for the cultural expression and exchange through which social identities are formed, and of access to the information and debate upon which democratic politics is founded.

Public television provides yet another legitimate institutional structure (in addition, of course, to the network of 'new' media discussed in the previous chapter) through which civil society may seek to influence/check government, support the values of the democratic culture, and thus strengthen the consolidation of democracy. Writing on western Europe where the idea of public service broadcasting is most mature, John Keane (1993) reminds us of its political significance: Here, he writes, public service broadcasting has been considered as a device 'for protecting citizens against the twin threats of totalitarian propaganda and the crass commercialism of market–driven programming and, thus, as devices essential to a system of representative government in which reasonable, informed public opinion plays a central mediating role between citizens and state institutions'.

Nevertheless the establishment of a public television station, just like the process of Taiwan's democratisation itself, was far from painless. In fact, all the cards seemed to be stacked against it, and for a time in the early 1990s it appeared that any planned public television station would become yet another instrument of government power. Indeed it seemed that the project would be abandoned altogether given the hearty resistance to this idea in many quarters. For one thing, the government and media 'experts' argued long and hard without ever reaching a consensus on how public service broadcasting might be defined (a problem not confined to Taiwan as the quotation from Britain's Peacock Committee at the head of this chapter demonstrates), gradually generating widespread disenchantment towards the divisive nature of the project. The situation was not helped by the way the three major parties – KMT, DPP and the New Party – politicised the issue and used it to score points off each other. In addition, the rise of the new media, a source of opposition politics since martial law was lifted in mid–1987, had already created a general sense of pluralism that extended beyond the political sphere and infected society, culture and the media. Opponents of public television criticised the way it seemed to negate the very idea of pluralism that the political opposition had been seeking for forty years. Yet pluralism was not the panacea its advocates would have us believe; evidence suggested that in fact the new media had introduced more complications to Taiwan's media landscape, including a wider scale of political involvement, more intensive commercial competition for ratings (markets treat people as consumers rather than citizens, and therefore have little respect for the political or social role of the media) and the pressure of media imperialism (see Chapter 3). In addition, cable television contradicts the notion that democratic citizenship is enhanced by a media system that is open to all regardless of income level (see Introduction). These problems gradually generated concern among Taiwan's intellectuals that the island still needed a genuine 'public' television institution that would empower viewers and allow them to determine their own agenda, instead of depending on politicians and media elites to set it for them: 'In broadcast news public persons are entitled to opinions, private persons experiences'. Public persons are routinely asked to comment on the news as worthy and legitimate representatives of a particular institution; on the other hand, private individuals stumble into the news, and become briefly newsworthy because of a unique experience they may have had. Together with particular genres, such as the staged debate, this kind of agenda setting affirms 'the power of the opinions of public persons and the powerlessness of the opinions of private persons' (Scannel, 1989). This powerlessness is demonstrated by the countless call–in television shows that now litter the schedules in Taiwan. One hour–long programme on TVBS describes itself as a call–in show, though it only gives its viewers twenty seconds each to deliver their opinions in the last five minutes of the programme. This provides neither the basis for genuine debate nor for genuine popular empowerment.

Moreover, where commercial television – and more so cable television – will deliver programming only to the most profitable geographic areas, or those areas willing and able to pay for such provision, public service broadcasting seeks to provide national programming (Scannel, 1989). After several years of wrestling with such issues, of their debate and review in the Legislative Yuan, the campaigns spearheaded by Taiwan's concerned intellectual community finally eased the passage of the Public Television Law in 1997 to provide high quality locally–produced programmes, but is not allowed to produce or broadcast news (*Friends of PTS*, No.1, pp.1-2).

This chapter suggests that a close examination of public television can provide another perspective from which to view the reform process, the transition to democracy, and the empowerment of civil society in Taiwan. The twists and turns that the project experienced reflected the shifts in attitudes towards the fundamental question: what does 'security' actually mean? As the domination of the security agenda by a state–centric approach dwindled, the sources of day–to–day insecurities derived from sub–state, trans–social patterns of threat perception have assumed added weight. This is the security of Giddens' 'life politics', understood as personal and social, and is a conception of security that returns the individual and the social group to centre–stage. On the one hand, the experience of insecurity in an age of 'globalisation' derives from a series of universal threats that do not respect geographic or political boundaries.

Famine, disease, terrorism, drugs, refugees are the most obvious and well–documented examples. But we might also add to this list the revolution in global communications and information technology transfers, and associated claims of an emergent mass global culture. States and societies often view these developments as a serious threat to their political and cultural sovereignty and try to limit their influence within their own borders. On the other hand the experience is also inherently local and personal: the threat to one's social–political identity, source of employment, source of food, basic needs and welfare provision, and to one's familiarity with the wider community and moral parameters, rather than the threat of war and the hegemony of alien ideologies that dominated security discourse before the end of the Cold War. In other words, we suggest that a close examination of Taiwan's public television history will also inform us of a new dimension to the studies of critical security that centralises the (normative and empirically–determined) notion of local/self empowerment.

The idea of public service broadcasting finds its roots in a long–standing debate that centres on whether the media and audiences benefit most from operating in a free market or a regulated system. Traditional liberal thought has pressed for anchoring the media to the free market to guarantee their security from government interference, though others (Jurgen Habermas, for example) have criticised this for eroding the quality of programmes. The commercial logic transforms mass communications into advertising, entertainment and public relations, damaging the critical faculties of the viewing public (Habermas, 1962). The 'public' are expected to be politically active only at (in)frequent intervals (elections, for example). Others have warned against substituting government power for corporate power.[5] In other words, one does not necessarily need to be a (neo–) Marxist (who would criticise the free market for commodifying culture and preventing the free flow of information because of structured power relationships and corporate influence) to question the liberal tradition from a security perspective: advocates of a free–market system seem to assume that the greatest threat to freedom derives from the state. They therefore make the same mistake as realists – ignoring the (growing) diffusion of (civil and corporate) power throughout society. This is most clearly defined in the media environment where economic power presents as big a problem for the champions of free media as government power:

> Based on the liberal conception of negative freedom (freedom*from* political authorities and state censorship), freedom of the press increasingly became a freedom wielded by owners of communication means rather than by citizens. The most important information became that which was profitable.

It was increasingly privatized and adapted to suit the interests and needs of those in power rather than the public (Splichal, 1994).

The most obvious consequence of this is that information can become subordinated to the interests of media *producers*, rather than its *consumers*. Moreover, business communities may have a financial stake in the media, thus restraining them from performing a watch–dog role that might threaten their corporate interests. Perhaps the business community is in close alliance with the government (to secure access to resources, financial and tax incentives etc.), again urging them to avoid close scrutiny of government activities. For example, Ben Bagdikian (1990), a close observer of the American media, has claimed that media conglomerates ignored official corruption in the Reagan era to 'protect a political ally', while Tunstall and Palmer (1981) have discussed the pursuit of 'regulatory favours' by the media in various European countries. Public service broadcasting seeks to redress this government/business influence and hand more power to civil society *without allowing government interference to grow as a consequence* (public service broadcasting has helped to 'decommodify' the media. Keane, 1991). This is important, for many critics of public service television observe that it promotes the negation of free media and encourages state interference. The funding of public service broadcasting is an unmistakable weak–spot in the model, providing governments with a powerful instrument of coercion over its activities. Peter Dahlgren (1995) discusses how the government of Sweden reacted to 'what it perceived as excessive left–wing perspectives in current affairs programming' in the early 1970s. 'The consequent "big chill,"' he writes, 'had a debilitating impact on independent, critical journalism for over a decade.'

Clearly balance is required, hence most public service broadcasters have looked to the British Broadcasting Corporation (BBC) as a possible model of organisation and finance (M. Rawnsley, 1998).[6] The BBC is particularly enticing for critics of the commercial mass media (such as Habermas) who lament the decline of a 'public' sphere due to the prevalence of 'market forces' (Garnham, 1983; Scannel, 1989). Commercialism has encouraged *homogenisation* (standardisation of formats) of output aimed at the largest audiences that occupy the middle–ground, rather than the *diversity* of programming so beloved by advocates of a free–market media. Yet even the BBC has been subjected to frequent pressure from the government of the day to conform to a political conception of the station's role, and the BBC is reminded that the finance it receives via the licence fee is not a natural right but a privilege granted by the representatives of the British electorate (see Negrine, 1994; 1996). Besides, it is difficult to escape the paternalism that seems to be inherent in the premise of public service broadcasting: commercial television produces programmes that are 'bad' for you; the state knows best and is determined to give audiences what is in their best interests. So the apparent elitism in deciding what constitutes public service broadcasting is a significant barrier to its democratic utility. Thus archetypal media mogul Rupert Murdoch is adamant that commercialism provides a public service: 'anybody who, within the law of the land, provides a service which the public wants at a price it can afford is providing a public service' (quoted in Keane, 1991).

The idea of balance conforms to Keane's 'general principle':

> communications media should not be at the whim of 'market forces' but rather placed within a political and legal framework which specifies and enforces tough minimum safeguards in matters of ownership structures, regional scheduling, programme content and decision-making procedures (Keane, 1991).

As Taiwan now knows only too well, putting this 'general principle' into practice is far from straightforward. The creation of a 'political and legal framework' must overcome many obstacles, the most obvious being the absence of ideological consensus among the political parties. A framework may also enact laws and regulations that contradict the interests of those political and corporate interests who enjoy a stake in maintaining the present system. In other words it is too easy to view Taiwan's flourishing public service television station as a success story, and thus overlook its tortuous progress from conception to reality.

State Control: From CPTV to PSB

In Taiwan the quality of television programmes declined with the creation of the third commercial station in 1969 primarily because of the explicit political involvement in the industry and the fierce competition between the three stations for viewers.[7] In this environment television continued to serve the specific political ends we outlined in Chapter 1, and these ends did not require the creation of public service broadcasting. After all, if the Republic of China on Taiwan was intended to be a showcase of democracy and the virtue of free–market economics that would attract western (American) support and serve as a model of development for mainland

China, how could the state justify financing a non–commercial television system? In early 1979 the ROC announced to its people that relations with the US had been severed, while on 1 March in the same year the American embassy in Taipei closed down. A renewed sense of patriotism swept through the island, reinforced by an elaborate government propaganda campaign that every day included the broadcast of a succession of anti–communist films. Variety shows were teeming with patriotic songs, while the intervals comprised propaganda slogans that reflected the new jingoism (Lee, 1979). Viewers, however, were not keen on the way ideology intruded on their daily entertainment; when the atmosphere calmed the television channels were inundated with complaints about this programming, but such outbursts of public displeasure had little real effect, and the system continued much as before. Clearly, public opinion had absolutely no bearing on Taiwan's social and political life before the onset of reform in 1987, and television producers ignored their consumers (Rawnsley and Rawnsley, 1998).

A group of academic observers led by Taiwan's leading authority on the media, Professor Lee Chan, were unimpressed with the apparent stagnation in the television industry, and during the 1970s they repeatedly called for the creation of a Public Service Broadcasting (PSB) television station to remedy the problems inherent in the current system (*United Daily News*, 14 April, 1992). However the KMT government ignored such demands. It simply could not risk upsetting the powerful interest groups that controlled the television industry and enjoyed close corporate ties to the KMT. Moreover the KMT claimed that there were no frequencies available for the creation of such a new station. The government was therefore able to justify not establishing a PSB on the grounds that it was restrained, first by higher authorities, and by considerations of 'national security':

> All broadcasting systems fall under government jurisdiction in at least one sense: Any authorized use of the frequency spectrum for broadcasting must be licensed by the government as a condition of belonging to the International Telecommunications Union (ITU), a United Nations body that attempts to keep users of the spectrum from interfering with one another (Browne, 1989).

The Executive Yuan claimed that the Ministry of National Defense and the Ministry of Transport and Communications controlled the frequencies assigned to the ROC by the ITU. Six had already been allocated to TTV, CTS and CTV, and one was retained for use by the government (*Min Sheng Pao*, 7 March 1987). The limited number of frequencies provided the government the perfect excuse to reject demands for new television stations – there were simply no spare frequencies. The government did overlook the fact that the Ministry of National Defense controlled a number of frequencies for their own use on the grounds of 'national security' and Taiwan's defence. Precisely how many they did control remained classified information, though it is clear that they exceeded requirements; frequencies granted to Taiwan by the ITU for sole use by television stations were procured by the military and security systems (Cheng *et.al.*, 1993). It was obvious to the champions of public service broadcasting that they would have to persuade the KMT government of the value of such a system, and thus encourage them to release a sufficient number of frequencies that might accommodate such a development. The difficulty was in persuading the government that the release of frequencies would not compromise national security. In a system if martial law based on the perception of a serious external threat from a major regional military power, this was far from easy. The advocates decided to underscore that a PSB would facilitate the government's idea of how television might play a significant role in Taiwan, and fulfil Sun Yun–suan's vision of the democratic and enlightening function of communications media in Chinese society:

> In addition to the existing three commercial television companies, we should establish a public television station which shall operate without advertisements, and be responsible for providing social and educational programmes in order to fulfil the needs of national education and government policy (Cheng *et al.*, 1993).

Premier Sun Yun–suan's words expressed his concern that for three decades, attempts to preserve China's 5000 year old culture had concentrated exclusively on education in Taiwan's schools. Like his predecessors Sun believed that television carried particular social and educational responsibilities, but criticised the three television channels for not living up to this vision. In 1982, Premier Sun instructed the GIO to remedy the situation by looking into the possibility of establishing a public television system (*Global Views Monthly*, May 1991). After two years of endless committee meetings within the GIO, transmission of the first public service programme on terrestrial television coincided with Chiang Ching–kuo's presidential inauguration, 20 May 1984. Up until this time the KMT government had rejected calls for PSB from advisers outside the state system, but once the Premier took a keen interest in the proposals, the wheels of Taiwan's intricate and often frustrating bureaucratic machinery began to turn much quicker than previously. Clearly the transformation of the television landscape, like democratisation itself, would be driven by political elites rather than by civil society. The inaugural broadcast was hardly inspiring: *Let us Read the Trimetrical Classics Together* was not destined to become a much loved and often repeated programme that was guaranteed to boost ratings figures. Nevertheless, its transmission on TTV was a landmark event in the history of Taiwan's media. Public service broadcasting had arrived (*Min Sheng Pao*, 17 May 1984).

Responsibility for such programming lay with a special task force within the GIO, but the government suggested that in keeping with the spirit of PSB it should move closer towards the public domain. However, it soon became clear that this decision was designed more to placate public and intellectual opinion and parade a more acceptable public face, than create a genuine public service broadcaster. In 1986, the task force was removed from the GIO and placed under the control of a private corporation, the Broadcast Development Fund (BDF), later becoming the Chinese Public Television or CPTV (*Min Sheng Pao*, 25 December 1986). However, the BDF was 'private' only in theory, and its organisation demonstrated the same kind of political involvement and overlapping responsibility that characterised the other television companies (Chapter 1). Thus the President of BDF was also the Director–General of the GIO, and his deputy was the BDF's Executive–Director. The President of the GIO's Domestic Department became the Director–General of Chinese Public Television, and his Deputy, Secretary, and the Presidents of the Programme and Executive Departments all came from either the GIO or the KMT's Department of Cultural Affairs (*Min Sheng Pao*, 2 February 1989; *China Times*, 17 December 1990; Pao Lee, 1993). The government was still in firm command: 50 per cent of CPTV's financial resources originated in the GIO, with the other 50 per cent obtained from a share of the commercial revenue earned by the three television stations (*China Times*, 18–19 May 1992).

Here is the explanation for the ingrained public scepticism in the viability of the project. Both the personnel and financial structures of CPTV suggested that the KMT machinery was intent on transforming this new television organisation into yet another instrument of government. The people were familiar with the tried and tested method of creating 'private' organisations, giving them different names and then staffing them with either members of government or government appointments. In this way CPTV fuelled the cynicism that greeted the prospect of an established Public Television Station in the 1990s.

Compared to the programmes produced and transmitted by the three commercial television stations, the themes and content of programmes made by CPTV could be described as 'more principled'. They were mainly designed to fulfil the educational and cultural void that Premier Sun had identified.[8] While CPTV struggled to boost its ratings in competition with the output of the other stations, it quickly acquired a following among the urban educated younger generation (GIO, 1985). This implies that CPTV was able to target its programming towards young professionals who played a significant role in the political, cultural and economic life of Taiwan, and who therefore might be influential in the future. Such policies would not have succeeded had CPTV not actually produce a number of high quality programmes; its programming offered more viewing choice for minorities (here defined as children, teenagers, and intellectuals) who were largely ignored by the ratings–driven commercial channels.

Yet CPTV was still criticised for avoiding subjects that the public were really concerned about or were interested in. As nothing more than an instrument of political expediency, CPTV evaded sensitive topics and vilified opinions it deemed contrary to the official line. This sensitivity was not confined to politics: in 1988 the station produced a pioneering series of programmes on sex education, *The Beginning of Human Beings*, but the production team decided to evade those themes that might offend the morality of the viewing public. The transmitted programmes lacked flair and imagination, and have been described as no better than a standard high–school textbook (*United Daily News*, 5 September 1988). Public affairs programming fared little better; they were often considered more pro–government than those transmitted by the three commercial stations (Cheng, *et.al.*, 1993). When CPTV did engage in investigative or critical television, they met with government disapproval and sometimes censorship. The GIO withdrew one of the episodes in the 1990 series, *Dialogue Between Wind and Grass*, because it 'exposed the problems relating to poverty and crime' (*Min Sheng Pao*, 8 July 1990). It is not surprising that CPTV's programmes were often dismissed as 'cheap propaganda' (Cheng, *et.al.*, 1993) that was not restrained by the 'hidden hand' of market forces. Moreover, programmes were dominated by the 'Chinese ideology' that had featured so prominently in the output of its rivals. Viewers wondered why CPTV spent so much money on producing dramas based on the ancient classics and avoided stories that focused on modern Taiwan. In November 1991, CPTV invested more than £320,000 on a ten–hours long series of documentaries about *The History of China* (designed to compete with the PRC's influential TV series, *River Elegy*).[9] At the same time, CPTV was willing to spend a mere fraction of the cost – £44,200 – on a six and a half hours documentary series, *Light in the*

Society, that discussed the character of Taiwanese society (*The Journalist*, 11 November 1991; Cheng, *et.al.*, 1993).

Demand for a genuinely public television system grew not because of the inherent bias against Taiwanese programming – that was an institutional given and an insignificant factor in the government's calculations. Rather, analysts realised that the financial basis for the organisation was sub–standard. CPTV was not a station: instead of transmitting its own programmes, CPTV had to requisition air–time on the three commercial channels. This meant that its programmes were often in competition with each other if they were shown simultaneously on more than one channel. This did not make strategic sense. In 1987, Premier Yu Kuo–Hwa agreed in principle that a public television station was needed, and so once again the GIO entered into a round of prolonged negotiations with other government departments for finance, land and frequencies (*Min Sheng Pao*, 7 March and 12 September 1987; *China Times*, 26 August 1987).

Determined to create a public broadcasting station the GIO was faced in 1985 with finding possible solutions to the scarcity of frequencies. One option was persuading the Ministry of Defense to release a number of its frequencies, and this was clearly preferred to requisitioning any of the existing commercial stations (which would have meant the government experiencing a serious financial loss. GIO, 1985). The Ministry of Defense objected to these proposals, suggesting that the release of frequencies would endanger Taiwan's security (*Min Sheng Pao*, 7 March 1987). Until the end of martial law, the military presented the most obstinate and powerful resistance to the creation of a PSB television station, and 'national security' was repeatedly invoked as justification.

Once Taiwan began to democratise, and the PSB project received the high–level support of President Lee Teng–hui and Premier Hau Pei–tsun, the military finally buckled under heavy political pressure. The Ministry of Defense agreed to release four frequencies for use by a future PSB station, and even provided a selection of land for the GIO to build upon (*Min Sheng Pao*, 3 October 1989; 24 May 1989). At the beginning of 1991 the new Director–General of the GIO, Shaw Yu–ming, announced that a new public service television channel, supervised by a politically–neutral committee, would soon begin broadcasting across the island (*Independent Evening Post*, 15 February 1990). Viewers were dismayed, however, to discover that when it referred to the creation of a public service television station, the government actually meant expanding CPTV. Audiences were quite unimpressed by the quality of CPTV programmes, its personnel structure and the way it was financed, all of which seemed at odds with the kind of system that would cater for the growth of a new civil society in a democratic Taiwan. Rather, the public now insisted that CPTV move away from GIO control and emerge, like a butterfly from a caterpillar, into a fresh, innovative, and above all *completely independent* television station. In the climate of political reform and the new mood of yielding to popular opinion, the government hastily abandoned plans to reorganise CPTV as a miniature GIO and instead created the Public Television Organising Committee (PTOC).

The Creation of PTOC

The story of PTOC parallels the growth of an active civil society in an increasingly democratic Taiwan. Not only did the government formulate the committee in the face of public pressure, but was forced into revealing the organisation process and the cast of characters who would shape PSB's future. The struggle between public opinion and the government's attempts to maintain its control through manipulation and secrecy was, at long last, forced into the open (*China Times Express*, 5 June 1990; *China Times*, 9 June 1990).

The list of committee members did indicate that there had been a radical break with the past: while the twenty–members of PTOC were still of the older generation of academics, they were at least not active in political parties (though the majority did support the KMT. *China Times*, 9 June 1990). Their reputation for honesty, efficiency and effectiveness in their own fields stymied any public criticism, and with his confidence boosted, Shaw Yu–ming announced that a public television station would be opened in three years (*Central Daily News*, 14 June 1990). As previous chapters have documented, the political and social changes also inspired the government to be more liberal towards the media, including public service broadcasting. It mobilised KMT members of the Legislative Yuan to approve the PTOC's budget in the 1992 session of the parliament provided two key conditions were met: (i) the members of the committees that would supervise both the PTOC and the envisaged public television station must be completely independent of the political parties. This was a radical departure from previous KMT practice; and (ii) PTOC should encourage and expand popular involvement in the project.

However, it soon dawned on observers that public service broadcasting was not a panacea for the media's problems: in fact, quality would come at a price, and that price might actually be *greater* political involvement. This is the essence of public television – avoiding the kind of problems that beset the commercial media. But without support for the kind of licensing system that funds the BBC – that is, guaranteed funding via taxation – the station would have to be funded completely by the government. Does this mean that the government would be able to scrutinise the work of the station? Would 'public television' simply become government property? Could the station establish the mechanisms and institutional checks required to monitor PSB without recourse to government? These questions became the source of renewed conflict between government, opposition and the burgeoning civil society.

Public opinion also influenced PTOC's programming. In fact, its management was keen to respond to surveys taken by the Gallop Organisation that found news to be the favourite programme for television audiences.[10] However, audiences were displeased with the prospect of PTOC producing only 3.2 per cent of programmes that would address Taiwan's social problems (especially when the 16 per cent of programmes on culture and art were taken into account[11]). For example in 1993, PTOC spent considerable money and energy in producing four documentary series: *Hong Kong, 1997*; *The Changes in the USSR*; *The European Community*; and *Chinese Abroad: Chinese People's Stories* (PTOC, 1993b). None were concerned with the remarkable social and political transformation that had enveloped Taiwan by the early 1990s.

To explain this many observers referred to what is known as the 'cultural bribery' theory (Fang, 1995). This describes a process whereby intellectual challenges to the social system are offset by promises to deliver high cultural programmes on a station designed specifically to meet the needs of the intellectual elite, a process that alienates the majority of viewers. The choice of programming was viewed as confirmation that the struggle between public demand and government control was set to continue. Critics also complained that Taiwan's media environment was facing insecurity due to its vulnerability to the revolution in international information flows that seemed to suggest the emergence of a mass global culture. Champions of PSB believed that it could help to make Taiwan more 'culturally' secure by preserving and promoting Taiwan's national identity. The problem surfaced when they tried to define 'national identity' – Chinese or Taiwanese? And what is 'Taiwanese' anyway? Should PSB provide more coverage of non–Han (ie. non–Chinese) programmes, or would dialect programming actually encourage further social division? More encouraging was the fact that PTOC's plans invited popular participation in its programmes through panel discussions and call–in shows, and proposed to divide its news output into regional and international divisions, thus demonstrating that positive centrifugal processes were at work.   Until this time, 'news' was something that happened only in Taipei! Wang Hsiao–Hsiang promised that regional news would 'concentrate on local politics, economics, and cultural developments ...'[12] Moreover, the public were invited to comment on the first draft of the Public Television Law in 1991.   Clearly PTOC – its organisation and programming – was making a significant contribution to the creation of a vibrant civil society throughout Taiwan that would now have a platform for expressing its opinions on a wide range of issues.   The people of Taiwan were fast becoming recognised as 'citizens' with a responsibility for the progress of democratic Taiwan.

Over the next two years, the Law was amended and redrafted several times to satisfy all parties.   While demonstrating the problems inherent in the system (the danger of institutional paralysis putting paid to 'good intentions') and delaying the creation of the station, this period was nevertheless important in galvanising civil society.   For example, scholars and students of journalism and communication at institutions around the island united in what became known as the 'People's Public Television Organising Committee' to present their own ideas and demands for the new station.   As their opinions were eagerly supported by the KMT's political opponents, this movement provides yet another example of how media issues become politicised.[13] Public opinion triumphed as all members of the government resigned from their positions within the PTOC (*China Times*, 16 and 19 March 1993).   Such (albeit isolated) episodes demonstrated the capacity, and therefore possibility, that a genuinely 'public sphere' with a public television station might be created in the future, *provided the social and political democratisation deepened to facilitate the strengthening of popular power*.   The public reaction to the possible derailment of the project ensured that the Public Television Law was finally passed in the Legislative Yuan on 31 May 1997, the bill's third reading.   The Public Television Station (PTS) began broadcasting on 1 July 1998.   Although the station was not allowed to make or broadcast news as Wang Hsiao–Hsiang had hoped for in the original plan, its vision of regional news provided the model for other channels which now divide their news output for particular audiences.

Politics versus Civil Society

'Public service broadcasting is driven by higher aspirations than solely to provide entertainment.   Public service broadcasting is the attempt to make

*quality popular programmes. It does justice to human experience. ... It
adds to the quality of people's lives. ...'*
– Keane (1991).[14]

While the construction of public television in Taiwan demonstrates the
growing power of civil society to sometimes act as a check and a balance
on the political system, we should be careful not to overestimate its
influence. The long and sometimes painful process of negotiation between
the government and opposition parties produced a compromised Public
Television Law: the GIO remains responsible for the station; none of the
commercial television stations have to pay towards PTS's operational costs;
once government funding ceases, PTS will have to become self–sufficient.
The solution satisfied everybody and nobody. However, the process did
confirm that democracy is all about discussion and negotiation. Hence the
possibility of political balance between the parties, and moreover the
possibility that the public can assume a far more active role in decision–
making processes.

Examining the history of public service broadcasting in Taiwan is
like reviewing the social changes from the 1980s to the 1990s. The KMT
was the main beneficiary of the three major television stations and
therefore did not want to disturb the status quo. So the government used
the media to preserve the Chinese ideology and fulfil policy needs. Even
though the government could spend in 1985 the equivalent of £7.3 million
on building an independent public service station, it vetoed the plan and
used one–fifth of the budget to establish the less public–oriented CPTV
instead. Described as a 'public service' provider, CPTV was in fact nearer
to being merely a vehicle of government propaganda. This was
unfortunate; its conservative agenda meant that it missed the opportunity to
record the radical changes that engulfed Taiwan in the final two decades of
the twentieth century.

Unprepared to remedy the defects of CPTV, it is clear that the
government was more concerned about its own narrow political interests
than the needs of Taiwan's media environment. However, in 1992 the
government felt compelled by the new social and political climate to
suddenly spend the equivalent of £106.9 million on establishing a new
public television station. The process was hurried, creating an organisation
that was less than ideal – PTOC – and plans to create a station were again
put on the back–burner. How can all this inefficiency be explained? After
all, the KMT had a reputation for state management of the free market
economy, and had built Taiwan into a world economic powerhouse.
Moreover, the organisation of television had, to date, been carried out with

maximum efficiency. Before the power of the KMT dwindled in 2000 the party–government was in an enviable position to do whatever it wanted when it wanted to do it. The problem, of course, is that 'efficiency' does not necessarily meet the needs of the public in a genuinely democratic structure. The needs of the public were defined by the KMT, and this corresponded with the style of management adopted by the government in all sectors of society. Further inefficiency was therefore inevitable. PTOC struggled because the population would simply not tolerate being cheated out of a genuinely public television station yet again by a government focused exclusively on its own political interests. The challenges that faced PTOC mirrored the growth of forces within Taiwan – political reformation, social movements, and a Taiwanese ideology. Public service broadcasting has also failed to overcome the evils of commercialisation, namely competition with other channels for viewers and the dependence on ratings as a measure of success. Neither can public service broadcasting provide programming for the broad church audience that its champions suggest. A perceived responsibility to remain balanced and objective – especially because of the threat of litigation and government pressure – cossets the audience from more the more politically and socially challenging programming that public service broadcasters claim they are committed to. Can any television schedule appeal to Nozick's 'visionaries and crackpots, maniacs and saints, monks and libertines, capitalists and communists and participatory democrats' (quoted in Keane, 1991) and avoid the kind of paralysis that is associated with such a conflict of interests? A more fundamental question is whether freedom of speech extend to 'crackpots' and 'maniacs', and should we make room for them in public service broadcasting if commercial television denies them a voice via the power of market forces? The bureaucracy of most public service stations that brought the BBC to the brink of destruction in the 1990s, and delayed the construction of any variation of the model in Taiwan for two decades, is likewise a serious threat. Can such institutions that straddle the political, corporate and civil society spheres and are, for the most part, beyond the scrutiny and control of the public, really be defined as 'public service broadcasters'? Does the very notion of public service contradict the technological and commercial nature of television (Dahlgren, 1995)? Can public service broadcasting allow public access to the media any more than other forms? The lesson is that the traditional conceptualisation of public service broadcasting represents an 'ideal' that is increasingly out of step with the modern media environment when it is thrown into an established competitive system (the BBC survives due in part to its status as the first television production company in the United Kingdom). Public service broadcasters must adapt or cease to exist; for many observers, it is that simple.

However, Taiwan now faces a new environment that not only presents a fresh series of fundamental challenges to the very conception of security, but also problematizes the organisation and function of the media. The opposition to public service broadcasting was predicated on the scarcity of frequencies in light of the needs of 'national security'. Just as Taiwan has finally been able to devote frequencies to public service broadcasting, the media have become subject to the pressures of globalisation. Globalisation implies that there are now no technological limitations on frequencies, and Taiwan's media face new international competitors who bring to audiences information and entertainment that is spatially and temporally limitless. Should Taiwan consider this cultural globalisation a threat or an opportunity? Moreover, how should governments deal with the apparent unaccountable nature of supranational institutions? There have even been calls for the creation of an international civil society and an international public sphere. Do these provide viable protection against the problems inherent in a globalised environment? It is to these questions we must now turn.

Notes

1. Chen has said that he will not change the name of the Republic of China to the Republic of Taiwan, will not call for a referendum to decide Taiwan's status, nor will he amend the constitution to reflect his predecessor's statement that negotiations with China can proceed only on a special 'state–to–state' basis. There have even been suggestions that Chen chose his outspoken and very controversial Vice President, Annette Lu, to be 'bad cop' to his 'good cop'. Lu is a well known and active critic of the PRC and champion of independence. These rumours have been fed by several of Lu's own pronouncements, and although Chen has denied such a strategy, it is possible that he chose Lu to placate the more radical wing of the DPP and maintain their support. Needless to say, Lu has claimed that the media has distorted her words, while in turn she has provided them with an exciting and dramatic series of stories. Her ability to maintain a high profile never ceases to astonish.

2. gio.gov.tw/info/98html/stat–e.htm

3. 'A genuinely consolidated democracy is perhaps best judged to be one in which the alternation of parties in power is regular and accepted' (Hall, 1993). The violence that occurred on the streets of Taipei following the 2000 Presidential election was directed at the KMT for having lost power; it was not designed to protest the result of the election. We can therefore conclude that Taiwan (including the military) accepted the result of the election, even though a significant number of voters (in fact, more than half of the electorate) were not happy with it.

4.   See the May 2000 issue of *Taipei Review* for interviews with key social movements and their assessment of what the election of Chen Shui–bian means for them.

5.   The debate has been particularly spirited in the US. See Kelley and Donway (1990), Holmes (1990) and Stepp (1990). Their ideas have also found champions on the other side of the Atlantic, where the British Broadcasting Corporation continues to defy the sanctity of commercial broadcasting. In particular, see Veljanovski (1989).

6.   The BBC is financed through a non–competitive system of funding. The BBC receives the whole of the compulsory licence fee levied on the mere possession of a television set.

7.   But this was not the kind of competition that is associated with market–forces. The television market was distorted by the fact that the three stations were owned or controlled by the various agencies of the state.

8.   According to Feng Chien–san (in Cheng *et.al.*, 1993), the CPTV spent an estimated NT$200 million (around £4 million) to 1993, providing more than 5,000 hours of programmes (including those purchased from abroad and co–produced with domestic production companies). However, these figures cannot be verified because, just like its commercial counterparts, CPTV did not reveal any official data. In contrast, CPTV has published a greater number of research papers about programming and audience analysis.

9.   'Written and produced by six intellectuals ... *River Elegy* was broadcast by the Chinese national television network in June 1988. It immediately caught fire, in terms of both popularity and controversy. The 'River Elegy' reformists, in powerfully emotional words, called for the total refutation and rejection of traditional conservative authoritarian Chinese culture ...' Chiou (1995).

10.   Interview with Hsiao–Hsiang wang, Taipei, February 1995. The results of the survey can be found in the Gallop Organisation's publication, *A Report on Audiences' Behaviour of Watching Television in Taiwan* (Chinese, 31 December 1991).

11.   This was a conservative figure, and represents only the proportion of self–produced programmes. Once imports were counted, the figure would be much higher.

12.   Interview with Hsiao–Hsiang Wang, Taipei, February 1995.

13.   Interviews with Dr Chung–Gen Chang (Taipei, December 1993); Dai–Hung Tseng (Taipei, December 1993); Chien–San Fang (Taipei, January 1995); Fu Hu (Taipei, April 1996).

14.   Keane here cites an interview with Jonathan Powell, former controller of BBC1, 2 November 1989.

5 Globalisation

'Globalisation, as a kind of myth of our times, is hard to grasp'
– A. Mohammadi (1997).

'We got the inspiration from the television series Baywatch, where lifeguards can mingle with the people'
– Jakarta police officer on a newly inaugurated bike patrol for which only 'good–looking and friendly' officers were selected (*Far Eastern Economic Review*, 20 July 2000).

We have now arrived at what we readily concede to be the most problematic part of our discussion. Our concern here is to query the relationship between the media, security and identity in Taiwan which arises from the (academically fashionable) process known as globalisation. Giddens (1990) defines globalisation as 'the intensification of world–wide social relations which link different localities in such a way that local happenings are shaped by events occurring many miles away and vice versa'. The problems derive from its mythical association that Mohammadi refers to in the above quotation. It seems to resonate with a mysticism that clouds any rational judgement of is appeal or application. For many it is a convenient catch–all term that lacks scientific basis.[1] The conventional approach, favourable among journalists and others who have not had the opportunity to subject such concepts to the rigorous examination they deserve, is to see globalisation as something of a utopia – a post–Cold War system where the 'end of ideology' and communications technologies create a more interdependent and culturally aware world. In Manuel Castells' (1997) lucid prose, globalisation is supposed to have subjected nationalism to a 'triple death' – the internationalisation of economics, a universal culture dissipated through a global media, and an 'assault on the very concept of nations'. Globalisation implies the decline, if not the eventual destruction, of the nation–state, and compromises four of its 'critical aspects', namely 'its competence; its form; its autonomy; and ultimately its authority or legitimacy' (McGrew, 1992). Optimists are confident that by making the international state system interdependent, globalisation has locked actors into a mutually beneficial, and inevitably secure framework. In short, the demise of the Cold War framework of international relations and the dawn of the much celebrated New World Order created an atmosphere of hopeful expectation that globalisation will facilitate international dialogue,

109

empower people and enhance security. The increase in shared interests and concerns that transcend sovereign borders has encouraged the growth of an international civil society: issues such as the environment, refugees, disease, human rights, famine and drugs are played out on our television screens each day and have motivated people to pressure their own and each others' governments for solutions.   Because the media have helped to decompress the world and bring global issues and events into our living rooms we are now more familiar with a whole encyclopaedia of nationalities than at any time in the past: Chechens, Bosnians, Tibetans, Hutus and Tutsis, Kurds, Palestinians, and hundreds more.   We are therefore more aware of their problems: whether the media activate a physical response to help them is another matter entirely.[2]   At the same time, because the problems these people face are 'news–worthy' they are frequently given a voice by the media.   The combined forces of globalisation and the information revolution have encouraged a worldwide and inclusive trend towards universal empowerment.   The Massachusetts Institute of Technology has led the way in promoting the possibilities opened up by the internet: Nicholas Negroponte speaks for many new idealists when he states that because of the internet, children of the future 'are not going to know what nationalism is.'   His colleague, Michael Dertouzos, agreed that the information revolution will facilitate 'computer–aided peace' that might 'help stave off future flare–ups of ethnic hatred and national break–ups' (quoted in *The Economist*, 19–25 August 2000).

However, recent history has demonstrated that there is also reason to be suspicious of globalisation and to be aware of its influence on 'critical security' at the beginning of a new century.   First, being locked into a mutually dependent relationship can have its downside; when one ship sinks, they all sink regardless of geography.   This is a particular problem in global financial markets where the value of one currency depends increasingly on another.   The impact of the 'Asian meltdown' on global financial markets and economies at the end of the 1990s affirmed that developments in one region – in this case Asia – have wide and serious international repercussions, and not just for the currency dealers; hardest hit by the crisis were ordinary Asians who saw their savings dwindle and their small businesses collapse.   Our critical security is threatened by forces that are beyond our immediate control, and are frequently beyond our comprehension.   The most worrying aspect is the feeling of powerlessness that such crises generate, the very opposite of the global emancipation promised at the end of the Cold War.

We should also be mindful that the nation–state survives (recall we stated in the Introduction that the nation–state remains an important means of political and social organisation):

> It survives administratively, at the level of iconicity, identity, defence, policing, education, and diplomacy, even if it must now compete with and is in part constituted by what may be a more prolific range of super–national and sub–national claims on national identity … (Barrett, 1997).

As *The Economist* (19–25 August 2000) has stated, 'The mistake people make is to assume that wars are simply caused by the failure of different peoples to understand each other adequately.' The real problem is that wars and crises are caused by individuals caught up in the state system; our critical security is threatened by the failure of politicians to understand a problem, to reach a workable solution or their hesitation in reaching a compromise with other governments to find a solution. Wars are started by intention, not misunderstanding, and usually by governments, not people. Relations between the two sides of the Taiwan Strait are usually referred to in terms of 'Beijing' and 'Taipei', in other words the seat of government and the centre of state activity. Better relations are hampered by the aversion of each government to discuss, negotiate, compromise at the same time that the number and variety of links between *people* on each side of the Strait are growing.

The legal, social and political frameworks in which the media operate are determined by the state. For example, the state decides the mix between private and public television; how the public media are financed; how different media systems are licensed; and imposes the barriers to unlimited free flow of information, entertainment and speech that might offend, defame or incite certain prohibited kinds of behaviour. This means the state continues to employ a range of methods by which they might control the media within their own borders, even in a 'democracy' that at the theoretical level encourages 'free' media (see Chapter 4). It also demonstrates the resistance of governments to supposedly 'universal' standards. The liberal tradition influenced the drive to link communications with universal human rights following the Second World War. Thus the Universal Declaration on Human Rights was adopted by the United Nations General Assembly on 10 December 1948, Article 19 of which stated:

> Everyone has the right to freedom of opinion and expression; this right includes freedom to hold opinions without interference and to seek, receive and impart information and ideas through any media regardless of frontiers.

Moreover, the UNESCO[3] Constitution of 1945 identified an explicit connection between freedom, security, peace, and the mass media, and the idea of the 'free flow of information' was adopted as its central principle. However, during the next two decades UNESCO and the idea of freely flowing information became subject to the turbulence of Cold War politics, as each side used propaganda, culture, and even education to promote their ideologies and attack each other. In this atmosphere the Declaration on Human Rights was interpreted in ways that corresponded to the political interests of each ideological bloc. Thus the Soviets protested American propaganda on the grounds that such activity contravened the principle of non–interference, while the US chanted the mantra of freedom of opinion, regardless of frontiers (Rawnsley, 1996). Information therefore became a political issue, and various conferences and summits were held to debate and revise existing conventions. Today the free flow of information continues to feature highly on the international agenda, with such forums as the Conference on Security and Cooperation in Europe (CSCE), the General Agreement on Tariffs and Trade (GATT) and the G8 summits devoting much of their time to discussion of these issues. The Final Act of the CSCE of 1975 held in Helsinki continued in the liberal vein started in 1948 by advocates of the Universal Declaration of Human Rights:

> increased cultural and educational exchanges, broader dissemination of information, contacts between people, and the solution of humanitarian problems will contribute to the strengthening of peace and understanding among peoples ...
>
> ... a wider dissemination of information contributes to the growth of confidence between peoples and therefore emphasize the essential and influential role of press, radio, television, cinema and news agencies and of the journalists ... The participating States [sic] aim to facilitate the freer and wider dissemination of all kinds, to encourage co–operation in the field of information and the exchange of information ...

It took the coincidence of three factors in the early 1990s – the end of the Cold War, the GATT Uruguay Round (the trade liberalisation talks), and the extraordinary revolution in information technology – to drive the momentum of globalisation. These three events contributed to freer flows in information, as well as goods, capital and technology. The Gulf crisis and war of 1990–91 demonstrated the effects of globalisation as information about the war sped instantaneously around the world faster than ever (Taylor, 1992). Even so, the normative and highly–principled visions will always remain difficult to implement when attitudes to the mass media and global information flows continue to be politicised and therefore subordinate to the interests of the state and the national economy.[4] The United States withdrew from UNESCO in 1984, ostensibly in protest against its financial incompetence and alleged corruption, but in reality because the prospect of a New World Information Order threatened American commercialism and free trade (Comor, 1997).

However, globalisation is a concept riddled with contradictions; not everything is black and white.   Even here we find anomalies that complicate how we assess globalisation, for the pressures that finally forced Taiwan's government to organise and regulate the chaotic cable industry were external in origin.   America threatened to impose trade sanctions if Taiwan did not prohibit its cable operators from infringing American copyright.   Moreover, the International Telecommunications Union (ITU) is a supra–national body with responsibility for overseeing the communications industry from a global perspective;   and we should not forget the unequal access to the shock–troops of globalisation.   Many poorer parts of the world are without the basic infrastructure that will give them access to the information revolution.   Even in those countries where the information revolution is most deeply embedded there is inequality as one must have access to a computer and know how to use it in order to access the information superhighway.   The internet is not the great force of democracy as many technophiles would have us believe.   A recent survey put the proportion of internet users as high as 35 percent, though their average age is 25, and they typically earn high wages (*Far Eastern Economic Review*, 3 August 2000).   A significant proportion of Taiwan is still alienated from the internet and thus do not have access to the kinds of democratic participation in political and social affairs that the champions of the World Wide Web like to boast about.   Thus the communications revolution has created a new global information underclass in a 'Fourth World' that is not defined by geographic territory.   This new underclass can live in New York, London, Tokyo or Johannesburg, as well as those areas of the globe conventionally and still conveniently defined as 'underdeveloped' (Castells, 1997): 'Two areas that exist directly alongside one another, or groups living in close proximity, may be caught up in quite different globalising systems, producing bizarre physical juxtapositions. The sweatshop worker may be just across the street from a wealthy financial centre' (Giddens, 1994).[5]

Cultural Imperialism

> *'Hello Kitty is cool. Mickey Mouse is not'*
> – *Taipei Times* (10 February 2000).

We would go further and suggest that globalisation has problematized the concept of identity that may impinge on how secure we feel we are. Far from breaking down cultural and national differences, globalisation and the spread of new communications technologies make it much easier than ever before to identify what separates people – to understand why 'we' are different from 'them'. It is a delusion to think that increased powers of communication will somehow bring us all together towards a more humane awareness and comparison (however, we emphasise that our position is a long way from Samuel Huntington's 1997 vision of a 'Clash of Civilizations' that oversimplified the connection between geo–political strategy and interests, and the emotional attachment to identity and culture[6]). Communications can add to knowledge, but not to encounter and experience. Technology has no power to do anything at all; the power of technology resides in the people who use it. Communications media remove the constraints on the possibilities for better international cooperation, but the greatest constraints are non-technical – political motivations, and our emotional beliefs which help us to filter out messages which do not correspond to our belief system and national parochialisms.

This is the crux of criticisms that are directed against 'modernisation theory', fashionable for a brief time in the 1960s. Following a paternal (some might say, colonial) agenda, the advocates of modernisation argued that communication could transform a traditional (that is, 'backward') society into a modern ('western–like') one (Lerner, 1963). This could be achieved because communications and the media socialise people, extend their horizons, and therefore stimulate them to want to transform their life–styles: 'The diffusion of new ideas and information stimulates the peasant to want to be a free–holding farmer, ... the farmer's wife to want to stop bearing children, the farmer's daughter to wear a dress and do her hair' (Lerner, 1963). In a similar way, modernisation theory provides an Orientalist's[7] view of how these processes are also at work in the political system, and drive the 'traditional' society towards adopting a 'democratic' method of organisation. Lerner explained how the media inform people of the world, encourage them to have political opinions, and then transform them into a fully participant army of citizens. Thus, 'the connection between mass media and political democracy is especially close' (Lerner, 1963). This is good news, for as more 'traditional' societies are transformed in this way, the security of the international system is guaranteed; for as all seasoned observers of international relations know, democracies do not go to war with each other (Huntington, 1991, has stated 'the spread of democracy in the world means the expansion of a zone of peace in the world. ... On the basis of past experience, an overwhelmingly democratic world is likely to be a world relatively free of international violence'). Tradition is 'bad', modernisation is 'good'. Moreover, modernisation theory was predicated on liberal market discourse and the free flow of information, and one finds in modernisation literature the ready use of such value–laden terms as 'democracy', 'freedom of expression', 'public watchdog'. However, many modernising states neglected to recall that the theory demanded the free flow of information (within and between countries) if the people were to embrace the vision of a better society. Rather many governments claimed that modernisation required them to suppress democracy rather than nurture it in order to limit the internal challenges to political and social stability that might threaten their development strategy. As happened in Taiwan modernisation provided an easy justification for the creation of media systems that were instruments of control rather than pluralism (see Chapter 1).

In response to the simplicity and ethnocentrism of modernisation theory, media and cultural commentators of the late 1960s welcomed what became yet another fashionable approach for understanding the modern world. 'Cultural imperialism' provided the theoretical framework for critics of the apparent domination of global information flows by the American media industry, American culture, and ultimately American values. This was viewed as an attempt by the United States to impose cultural, economic and political hegemonies on the world after the Second World War. 'Modernisation' of developing countries encourages their dependence on an essentially exploitative set of economic relations, and its central argument has been summarised (as recently as 1998, though the height of cultural imperialism frenzy was the mid–1970s) in one sentence by Herbert Schiller (1998): 'Today, the United States exercises mastery of global communications and culture'. Cultural imperialism provided the pretext for the defence of 'Asian values' that continues to lend justification to many of the undemocratic management strategies of several states in the region, particularly Singapore (Diamond and Plattner, 1998).[8]

These ideas appreciate that the media are bound up in a complex set of power relations and can thus assume the kinds of political roles that have been discussed in this book. They are also concerned with a conception of security that implies the importance of maintaining national sovereignty. Nevertheless the cultural imperialism thesis lacks credibility in a world where information flows are multi–directional and cultures are often hybridized (Sreberny–Mohammadi, 1996; Giddens, 1991). Today, more nations of the southern hemisphere are producers of global media products as they are receivers. The impact of 'Bollywood' – fusing the indigenous culture with western styles to produce a unique (and extremely popular) film production machinery – would seem the most obvious example, while the influence of Asian film directors such as Akira Kurosawa, Ang Lee and John Woo has been felt in Hollywood.[9] By the end of the 1980s, *TV Globo*, Brazil's main television network, exported its *telenovelas* (a form of soap opera) to 128 countries, many of which were outside South America (including China, the former Soviet Union and East Germany. Tracey, 1988). Indeed television provides numerous examples of 'reverse cultural imperialism': Brazil to Portugal, Latin America to the United States (Antola and Rogers, 1984). Taiwan (and for that matter, South–East Asia) is currently experiencing cultural and other influences that originate in multiple centres of globalisation – the US, Japan and mainland China. Japan is America's main competitor as Taiwan's source of such products. Its enormous economic power makes Japan the largest producer and exporter of information, goods, technology and capital in Asia. Meanwhile retailers throughout the region are now targeting a new breed of consumer – twenty–somethings with high incomes and money to burn, and who have 'become far more Asian in their tastes':

> No longer is the United States regarded as a source of inspiration and no longer are Americans seen as the embodiment of success. ...
> ... The prescriptions of the International Monetary Fund, which was generally seen as an agent of US government policy [during the Asian financial crisis] were widely perceived as high–handed and exploitative. ... Rightly or wrongly, disillusionment with the US ... has seen consumers in Asia increasingly rejecting products and services thought to represent America, and instead turning to Asia, and especially Japan, for their inspiration. ...
> The US multinationals that expanded so visibly into Asia over the past 10 years will suffer unless they can reinvent their images and be seen as locally oriented companies. And to a far great extent, the next Asian spending boom ... will be led by Asian brands selling strongly in Asian markets (*Far Eastern Economic Review*, 15 June 2000).

For the moment, Taiwan remains a key destination for cultural products from Japan. In fact, the island is influenced by Japan in ways that go beyond the import of television programmes and computer technology (in Taipei, cable companies offer at least three channels dedicated to Japanese news, cooking, soap opera and game shows): The younger generations are obsessed with Japanese *Manga* comics and *Pokémon*, while young girls spend most of their money on copying the latest fashions of their Japanese counterparts and idolising Japanese pop singers. A headline in the English–language *Taipei Times* (10 February 2000) captured the essence of this trend: 'Taipei youth say Japan hot, US not'. Taiwan is unable to compete with such phenomena on a regional basis. With one or two exceptions – the television drama *Judge Bao*, for example, that dramatises the exploits of a legendary Chinese magistrate – television programmes produced in Taiwan are not popular anywhere else in Asia.[10] The fundamental question is whether this is a different form of cultural imperialism: Is the 'Japanization' of Taiwan any more or less preferable than 'Americanization'? Or are we in fact seeing the creation of a hybrid culture, one that defies easy categorisation, that expresses a post–modern Taiwanese identity?

The criticisms of the uni–directional flow of information that the school of cultural imperialism identifies are given added weight by recent ethnographical research on the alleged personification of cultural imperialism, Coca–Cola, Disney, and especially McDonald's, that suggests the importance of localising influences. Nations hesitate before embracing these symbols of American life, and will do so only when the corporation itself responds and adapts to the society in which it seeks to operate. For example, before entering the Asian market, McDonald's was just a normal fast-food chain outlet in the US, where the corporation and American consumers entered into a tacit agreement that the former would provide cheap and relatively decent food, while the latter would finish the food quickly and leave. But McDonald's realised that in order to succeed in Asia, particularly in Taipei, Beijing, Hong Kong, and Tokyo, they must revise their operational attitude, and thus the agreement between consumers and the corporation breaks down. By providing clean toilets, non-interrupted space for consumers, and by becoming involved in local society (for example, the organisation of birthday parties for children), McDonald's has become one of the most popular businesses in these foreign cities. In other words, a broad interpretation of McDonalds' success suggests the power of globalisation; but upon closer examination, it is the element of localisation which is more influential. For the interaction to succeed, both sides – corporate and consumer – must compromise their behaviour and expectations (Watson, 1997). This is neither globalism nor localism, but Tu Weiming's 'glocalism'[11] resonating through the discourse. 'In the realm of popular culture', writes James Watson:

it is no longer possible to distinguish between what is "local" and what is "foreign". Who is to say that Mickey Mouse is not Japanese, or that Ronald McDonald is not Chinese? To millions of children who watch Chinese television, "Uncle McDonald" (alias Ronald) is probably more famous than the mythical characters of Chinese folklore.

The case of Taiwan pushes us towards viewing identity as a fluid concept, as something that shifts over time and according to different situations. Thus one can be 'Taiwanese' when watching the local news from Taipei; from the Republic of China when watching news of threats to Taiwan by the PRC; Chinese when tuning into Mandarin–language cable broadcasts; a citizen of the world when watching CNN. Our viewer does not shed his Taipei, Taiwanese or Chinese identity at any point in this process. Within himself he is each of these and all of these. The modern media allow viewers to move vertically from level to another without them ever having to leave the comfort of their own armchairs. This is a post-modern pluralist concept of audience identity which breaks down the political barriers of 'either/or', and has only been meaningful to Taiwan since the growth in popularity of cable programming (the cable penetration rate in Taiwan is 80 percent, the highest in the Asia–Pacific region). But again, political barriers stand in the way. The explosive combination of a Presidential election, missile tests, and the American Seventh Fleet steaming into the Taiwan Strait in 1996 forced identity back onto the agenda; it was a political and social issue which the media naturally seized upon and reported. Media coverage accentuated identity, and the differences between the PRC and the ROC were again highlighted. The problem is that Taiwan's media prefer to present a simplified and easily digested black and white image of otherwise complex issues, and issues do not come more complex than cross–Strait relations. In the rush to print the latest rumours and speculation about the mainland and its intentions towards China, newspapers will avoid context and background that would give the story the required depth and facilitate understanding. This is important for understanding how the consumers of news in Taiwan view and understand cross–Strait relations.

Appreciating that identity is fluid, neither spatially nor temporally bound, also helps us to understand a little better the flaws in the 'cultural imperialism' thesis. Yes, Taiwan has been subject to American cultural influence, but through the centuries it has also been subject to Portuguese, Japanese and of course Chinese cultures (while the US has itself imported cultures and political practices). Identities and cultures do not replace one another as the cultural imperialism thesis would have us believe. Herbert

Schiller's (1969) argument, that what is at stake 'is the cultural integrity of weak societies whose national, regional, local or tribal heritages are beginning to be menaced with extinction by the expansion of modern electronic communications' is misplaced. Rather identities coexist. In fact, some observers of Taiwan's media output have witnessed the striking preservation of traditional values and Confucian ethics despite globalisation (Chen, 1998). We should also be encouraged by the way globalisation has facilitated the creation of an international civil society. While the nation–state will never 'whither away' – it is still a useful method of organising political society at both international and domestic levels – global media flows help to show audiences that they share problems and should work together to find solutions. Thus Greenpeace transmitted video footage by satellite to promote an international disapproval of nuclear testing in the Pacific and the dumping of an oil–rig in the Atlantic. Meanwhile, the internet was used to mobilise protests against capitalism in 1999 and 2000, and reports have circulated that similar protests, again organised in cyberspace, will mar the 2000 Olympics in Australia. Amnesty International has regularly enticed the media to cover stories that win international sympathy for their causes.[12] The global media help to localise the global (the environment, poverty, disease, etc.) while *at the same time* globalising the local (Rwanda, Bosnia, East Timor, and of course Taiwan). Certainly the (admittedly limited) media flows between China and Taiwan reflect the multiplication of exchanges on other levels via the 'reactivation' of 'economic, social and cultural networks' (Mengin, 1999). This has given rise to a form of international or, more accurately, cross–Strait civil society based on long standing forms of identification. For example Mengin (1999) details the success of Taoist networks that not only link Taiwanese and Chinese, but also form a kind of 'economic community'.

The spectacular failure of UNESCO to overcome the problems of cultural imperialism, and guarantee that local cultures were not displaced,[13] prompted many societies to adopt coercive methods of controlling the flow of information. This is the method favoured by nations who wish to jealously guard and preserve their national identities and do not have sufficient faith in the power of identity to resist displacement. Those who oppose the global information village in this way are merely substituting one form of cultural imperialism for another, giving rise to a more fragmented and protectionist global order. Examples of this in practice were provided in the Introduction (p.6), and they continue today in many areas of the world.[14] Identity is considered to be rigid, something that has been politically decided should not be altered or threatened in any way. So what needs to be addressed is just how far societies open up to globalisation while taking active measures to protect and preserve their identities? What mechanisms will allow this to work without sealing the society from all outside influences? Several societies in the Middle East that have allowed satellite dishes to mushroom have tried to regulate their use via MMDS (multichannel multipoint distribution system). This enables governments to filter out programming of which it does not approve, and the security of the nation–state clashes with the critical security (empowerment and freedom) of the people (Sreberny, 2000). The internet revolution has presented new challenges to governments' attempts to regulate the flow of information and opinion. In 1996 information officials from member governments of the Association of South East Asian Nations (ASEAN) gathered in Singapore to discuss the problems posed by the emergence of cyberspace. While their main concern was the easy provision of and access to pornography, they also expressed anxiety that the internet would ease western cultural imperialism and threaten 'traditional values'.[15] At the close of the meeting the officials 'affirmed the importance of having safeguards against easy access to sites which run counter to our own cherished values, traditions and culture,' but they failed to agree on a uniform ASEAN solution. Instead, each government would deal with the problem in their own way – for good or bad.[16] So in many respects we can see how globalisation has strengthened, rather than weakened the resolve of sovereign states, and the way they make the intellectual and political connection between globalisation and critical security determines whether they see this phenomena as a challenge or an opportunity.

Media Glocalism

Nevertheless, there is cause for optimism. A significant proportion of modern culture – film, music, television news – has been internationalised, but media systems on the whole remain local. American television programmes may dominate the schedules in some, indeed many, countries, but research has suggested that they are rarely the most popular *where sufficient local programming of comparable quality exists* (Straubhaar, 1997; Morley and Robins, 1989).[17] This is also the case in Taiwan's lucrative magazine market, where such international women's magazines as *Cosmopolitan*, *Elle* and *Vogue* have launched Chinese editions. However, locally owned women's magazines, such as *Beauty*, *Lady Ann* and *Mademoiselle* remain the leaders in the domestic market.[18] Similar evidence also points to the fact that the lack of serious investment in Taiwan's film industry has encouraged the popularity of American films.[19]

The example of the Korean film industry, rejuvenated in 1999 after the removal of quotas on Hollywood films (under pressure from the US who claimed such protectionism was anti–competitive), provides a promising model of how investment, originally designed to allow Korean films to combat Hollywood, can generate quality and may revive a failing industry (*Far Eastern Economic Review*, 20 July 2000). In fact, there is a significant body of comparative research that demonstrates most television programmes in the 'mass' media (as opposed to cable) are produced nationally, rather than imported (Bens, *et.al.*, 1992). Most of the foreign programmes that are imported into Taiwan and elsewhere are English–language and thus reach only a small elite or the expatriate community with access to cable television. (The main foreign channels available via cable in Taiwan include the Japanese channel NHK, Disney, Discovery, and HBO, AXN, Sun Movie and Cinemax for twenty–four hours movies. All of these feature Chinese subtitles. CNN can also be received though without the option of Chinese subtitles.) Moreover we must be mindful that these audiences indigenise foreign programmes in the way they interpret them and give them a meaning that is relevant to their own experience (see, in particular, the pioneering work of Liebes and Katz on the American television series *Dallas*, 1990).[20] Foreign entertainment programmes are popular in Taiwan, especially among the young, but only if they have been tailored for the Taiwan market (including dubbing or subtitling into Mandarin). Programmes which are produced by Taiwan–based companies and offering local news remain more popular than imported programmes or specialised programmes offered by international media companies (*Free China Review*, February 1996). Hence the Murdoch Corporation soon realised that if it wished to compete with indigenous programming in the Chinese–speaking world, it had to provide a Chinese–language schedule. Hence Star TV devoted one of its Asian channels to Mandarin–language programming. The success of Star TV in Taiwan demonstrates that targeting a specific language audience can enable foreign media corporations to compete with domestic programmes (Chan, 1997). In turn, Taiwan's domestic television industry has been provoked by the competition with Star TV into producing better quality programmes (especially entertainment).

Nevertheless, a globalisation that is combined with global capitalist forces threatens to ignore Taiwan's minorities, to subdue them under media products that are formed by commercial considerations. Therefore any definition of the 'Taiwan market' must embrace the diversity of local cultures that co-exist on the island; and, more important for identity, it is important to speculate how Taiwan's minorities will be affected by globalisation. If these minorities are assimilated into a greater 'Taiwan' identity that will allow the island's media to compete with foreign media products, their experience of being part of the global society will be enriched. A more integrated approach to identity will strengthen Taiwan's media, and will therefore allow the domestic industry to respond to foreign programming.

An effective response to the pressures of media imports depends upon providing quality local programming (this was Iran's reluctant response to the appeal of television imports. Mohammadi, 1997). But quality is difficult to define and measure. Quality requires financial resources, the availability of talent, and the willingness of the media to take risks and shift from merely satisfying the middle ground. These are all difficult to attain in a media environment that is characterised by a proliferation of channels eating up audiences and resources. Tu Weiming (1996) has expressed concern about this very issue:

> As the old ways of exercising bureaucratic and ideological control over the public sphere are abandoned ... experiments dictated by the supply and demand of the market economy dominate the cultural scene. An uninterested consequence of democratization has been the collapse of some highly respected and seemingly enduring cultural institutions ... With politicization and commercialization, all cultural traditions have become vulnerable.

Such apprehension has been justified by research which showed that in 1996, one-third of 68 local cable channels in Taiwan offered only locally-made programmes. However, around half showed no local programmes at all. Of 119 system operators, most offered less than three hours of local programmes per day. The little they did provide were described as low budget productions of mainly variety shows, soaps and news (*Free China Review,* February 1996).

If nothing else, the fear (real or imagined) of a cultural invasion should stimulate the demand for better programmes. Perhaps the solution lies in ensuring that the revenue accumulated through middle–ground programming is reinvested in the production of quality output. There is reason to be optimistic: recent successes for Taiwan–made movies at international film festivals, together with a noted revival of interest in opera, traditional and experimental theatre and dance, are positive signs that there is an appetite for serious culture in modern Taiwan (Gold, 1996; *Free China Review*, September 1998). Moreover globalisation has intensified the importance of developing a sufficient public television system that can manage the new problems it creates. As the previous chapter discussed public television holds out the promise of anchoring in society a more secure definition of identity that embraces the interests of demographic minorities. That Taiwan's PTS has so far been far from satisfactory in providing a response to globalisation has prompted a group of prominent academics led by Feng Chien–san to campaign for the introduction of more public television stations (or, more accurately, 'deprivatized and professional management of TTV and CTS'. *Taipei Times*, 29 May 2000).[21]

Regionalism

> *'The original model of a pan–Asian, one–size–fits–all programmer – where Hollywood blockbusters could be beamed to television viewers from Heilonjiang to Hyderabad – is in tatters'*
> – *Far Eastern Economic Review* (27 July 2000).

The best way to understand Taiwan's media is through the forces of regionalism rather than globalisation. This idea assumes a new multi-polarity, based on regional blocs. Joseph Straubhaar (1997) has discussed at length the regionalisation of television flows based on distribution, while Annabelle Sreberny (2000) has provided a fascinating insight into regional media flows in the Middle East. One might also note that geographic neighbours are now organising structured regional responses to global media flows. The best example is the Arab Satellite Communications Organization (ASCO) which, although beset by the kinds of problems that challenge all supra–national institutions (see Negrine, 1997), nevertheless bring together sovereign states in an attempt to meet the communications needs of the Arab world, including the launch of the Arabsat satellite system in 1985. We might also consider the Palapa regional system that links Indonesia, Malaysia, Thailand, Singapore and the Philippines. In 1993 Hong Kong's TVB joined with Taiwanese interests to form TVBS, producing programmes that were relayed to Taiwan using the Palapa satellite and then redistributed using cable (Chan, 1996). Enjoying a 100 percent share of cable subscribers in Taiwan, TVBS (later joined by the news channel TVBS–N) remains one of the most popular channels in Taiwan today. At the end of the 1996 meeting of the ASEAN[22] Committee on Culture and Information, participant countries accepted the need to organise on a regional basis, and thus decided to launch an ASEAN website, satellite channel, a biannual arts festival, and a Youth Friendship programme. Taiwan launched a commercial satellite (ST–1) in August

1998 as a joint venture between Taiwan's Chunghwa Telecom and Singapore Telecom. With a footprint that covers China, India, Indonesia, Japan, Malaysia, the Philippines, Sri Lanka and Singapore, the satellite has much potential in helping Taiwan to become a regional media player (*China News*, 4 August 1998; *Free China Journal*, 4 September 1998).

However we believe that Taiwan fits a slightly different model, a regionalisation based on language and culture rather than geography, so Taiwan's media industry has so far concentrated on striving to be a major player in the production and export of Chinese–language programming. Thus in 1995 the government of the ROC launched a capital–intensive programme to transform Taiwan into an Asia–Pacific media centre. This was based on research conducted by the GIO that discovered Taiwan's output of Chinese–language film and television in the Asia–Pacific region accounted for 47 percent of the total (the figures for Hong Kong and China were 28 percent and 25 percent respectively). Clearly there were opportunities here for Taiwan to build its position as a leading player in the region's media landscape, particularly as Hong Kong, the previous centre of Chinese–language programming was due to be handed back to the PRC in 1997. The intention of this project is to develop a regional Chinese–language media industry (the first phase concentrated on the motion picture and television industries; the second phase, which began in 1998, aims to create the framework that will encourage the production of Chinese–language media, including print). Thus the title of the project is something of a misnomer, as it cannot hope to represent the Asia–Pacific region if it is concentrating only on Chinese–language media. It is likewise interesting to note that a 1999 report on the project identified the 'English communication skills of ROC citizens' as a 'weakness', suggesting that Taiwan is still not confident that it can be a leader in the Chinese media market *without* having to depend on English.[23] We can therefore conclude from these facts, plus the sluggish and hesitant development of the project that other political motives lay behind it, and that the Asia–Pacific media centre is merely wishful thinking or the rhetorical flourish of a government still locked in political competition with the PRC.

Nevertheless, such developments do bring to the surface the question of how the identities of the so-called Overseas Chinese are affected by globalised media. Are their identities actually strengthened by their incorporation in this global culture? Perhaps regionalisation is a valuable way of thinking about the many media which serve to keep the Chinese diaspora in touch with home. It also reinforces the idea of shifting identities, no longer spatially or temporally bound – the media allow audiences to experience their local, national, regional and even international identities. The coexistence of identities has been made easier by globalisation and by the communications/transport revolutions. Greater assimilation and generational differences are no longer serious barriers to being part of the wider Chinese community.

Where is the geographic centre(s) of popular Chinese culture? Taiwan and Hong Kong media have dominated the Chinese–language market, and are marching towards the idea of serving 'Greater China'. Chan (1996) has called Greater China a 'geocultural' construct, 'in that the common cultural context of its television output is more fundamental than the difference in language. ... Both the past and the future of these ... countries are intertwined with each other, and such cultural affinity has served as a positive factor in the formation of a Greater China television market'. Meanwhile, in an article published in 1993(b) Thomas Gold identified the significance of cultural flows from Taiwan and Hong Kong to the mainland; and since 1995, the Information Broadcasting Company (a service established by the Cheng Sheng Broadcasting Corporation) has been using ISDN technology to simulcast with KAZM AM 1300, a Chinese–language radio station in Los Angeles. Before then, Taiwan concentrated on the export of its programmes to overseas Chinese on video cassette, though in 1993 it began to transmit programmes via satellite operators in North America. In February 2000, the government of the ROC announced the launch of a special Chinese–language satellite television station aimed solely at the Overseas Chinese and broadcasting news, entertainment, films and government policies (*Taipei Times*, 10 February 2000).

Thus Taiwan is a major player in the regionalisation and the globalisation of Chinese culture *though only among the Chinese disapora*, and many organisations exist to promote Taiwan and its interpretation of what it means to be Chinese overseas. While its news agencies are unable to compete with the giants in the market, such as Reuters and Associated Press, they do at least provide a source of news and information about Taiwan to the world's media. The Central News Agency (CNA) provides daily information to over 100 Chinese–language newspapers worldwide. It also offers English–language news to foreign media and Spanish–language news to media in Latin American countries. Its website is one of the most visited by foreigners seeking information about Taiwan. Many of Taiwan's newspapers also have established internet editions. Some are in English, but most are in Chinese, providing yet another portal for the Overseas Chinese to keep up with developments in Taiwan and China. The Central Broadcasting System transmits radio programmes in seven dialects, including Southern Fukienese, Cantonese, Hakka, Mongolian, Tibetan and

Mandarin; Radio Taipei International broadcasts in eleven languages worldwide, while the Voice of Asia broadcasts in English, Mandarin, Thai and Indonesian. The latter station hopes that 'understanding between Asian people and nations can be gained and communications between foreign labourers and their families and relatives at home can be conducted' (*Voice of Asia Information Pamphlet*, GIO). The language policies of these radio stations demonstrate that mainland China (including Tibet) and south–east Asia are the priority target audiences – again regional in contrast to global. The Voice of Asia is especially popular with mainland audiences who welcome its non–political programming. Its propaganda value is therefore clear.[24]

Conclusions

> '*I grew up as a Japanese during the colonial period, became a Chinese under the KMT, and may die as a naturalized American, but in heart and soul I have always been a Taiwanese*'
> – Taiwanese in the US, quoted by Wu (1996).

Globalisation and transnational media flows have direct consequences for critical security. For one thing they have brought to the surface the relationship between the media and identity as never before. Should globalisation be considered a threat or a welcome opportunity? Is Taiwan's identity secure now that it is a full democracy? Many states have tried to use globalisation as a means to perpetuate their existence and the continuation of coercive or authoritarian practices. In many respects globalisation has guaranteed the survival of the nation–state as the last bastion of resistance against cultural invasion. This implies there is no escaping the influence of globalisation. The world is smaller than ever before, and while societies might resist globalisation, they cannot escape its force entirely. In Taiwan, the legalisation of cable television was due in part to the fact that illegal receivers could already pick up spill over signals from overseas satellites and television stations (including Chinese Central Television, or CCTV). Identities will not be extinguished, but will either become accentuated or acquire a fluidity that will provide the basis of co-existence. While the political response to globalisation will be of major significance, it is also crucial that Taiwan's media reassess their own riposte. This requires a greater concentration of effort and resources on the quality, rather than quantity, of media products, and intensifies the need to restructure the television industry (especially public television) as an effective response. In this way, the national and local identities that are so cherished by opponents of cultural imperialism will be preserved, while allowing audiences to participate fully in the global media society.

The media – local or international enjoy a tremendous capacity to either frighten people and cause them to fear for their lives (without, it might be added, a single shot ever being fired), or encourage them to feel relieved that crisis has been avoided, usually through a much–celebrated aptitude for statesmanship, if not brinkmanship. We discussed in Chapter 1 how such security considerations determined the KMT's control over the media in Taiwan before the decision to democratise was taken. But considerations of national security remain high on the agenda. Reports in the domestic and overseas media in the long run–up to the 1996 and 2000 Presidential elections cited warnings from Chinese officials to Taiwanese against voting for the 'wrong' (ie. pro–independence) candidate. Although the intimidation did not work during either election (and especially in 2000), we cannot ignore the fact that such media reports sent ripples of panic through the island. In fact, coverage of the military's perception of the China threat so saturates the media at such times that the more cynical among us are left wondering whether the media are used by certain elements in Taiwan to play up a threat for political and economic gain (just as certain revisionist theories of the Cold War explain its continuation for forty years by close examination of the military–industrial complexes on both sides of the Iron Curtain). Conspiracy theory aside, it is more likely that Taiwan's media just fail to understand China and prefer to report rumours and uncorroborated 'facts' without also supplying the background that would enable to consumer of the news to place it in context. If we add to this the fact that the international media will focus on the dramatic (the cross–Strait) implications of the elections, rather than the elections themselves, then the security consequences are magnified. Consider for example how international concern for the implications for China of the 2000 election prompted American journal *Newsweek* to refer to Chen Shui–bian as 'Beijing's worst nightmare'. Television pictures of crises – whether from Taiwan, Bosnia, Haiti or East Timor – are often said to drive the foreign policy agenda of 'western' governments, particularly the United States. The government is therefore forced to respond to or anticipate the public pressure that such media coverage will generate, though whether the so–called 'CNN effect' is a fact or fiction is still the subject of intense debate among scholars of the media and international relations (Taylor, 1997; Negrine, 1996). Many books and articles have been written discussing whether the United States' decision to send war–ships into the Taiwan Strait during the 1996 crisis made conflict with China more or less likely. The danger is that the American population will begin to wonder why their country risks being dragged into somebody else's war – the Gulf War did not 'kick the butt of the Vietnam syndrome once and for all', as the American military and Bush administration hoped (Taylor, 1992). A local problem has the capacity to soon escalate into a regional, if not a global problem. For Taiwan, however, this focus on cross–Strait relations and diplomacy is a particular challenge, for it disguises the other problems that exist at the level of *critical* security. Thus such global concerns as AIDS, the environment, drugs and terrorism are often overshadowed by an almost exclusive concentration on relations between Taipei and Beijing. Greater incorporation in the global news village will begin to remedy such problems.

Meanwhile the internet presents its own challenges to security. Largely beyond structured regulation, the flow of information and opinions through cyberspace permeates national borders and circumvents state sovereignty as no other medium, our earlier reservations about its *democratic* value notwithstanding. After all, the internet can be a force for education, cultural exchange, a forum of communication between otherwise marginalised groups, and a vehicle of political dialogue. However, the internet can also spread vicious rumours, uncorroborated 'facts', hate and racism, sickening pornography, and education on how to build weapons that can wipe out a whole school, as in Columbine in 1999. E–mail viruses can fell a global computer network in hours, while the threat of hackers has endangered the growth of e–commerce. Companies are having to find ways to deal with new threats to corporate security and design elaborate systems to protect networks against viruses and hacking. Governments too are investing huge amounts of money into developing computer systems that will resist terrorization from cyberspace. In theory anonymous hackers have the ability to paralyse a state from the other side of the world. Meanwhile the internet has become another tool in the continuing propaganda wars around the globe ('Hackers attacked the website of Burma's military rulers, forcing its to shut down. A group calling itself X–Org posted slogans on the site demanding democracy.' *Far Eastern Economic Review*, 17 August 2000). Following the furore in 1999 over President Lee Teng–hui's claims that negotiations with China should proceed on a special 'state–to–state' basis, Chinese hackers entered government and academic computer networks in Taiwan to leave messages that reaffirmed China's claim of sovereignty over the island and warning against independence. Similar incursions have occurred in the other direction: The next day, a hacker in Taiwan entered Chinese government websites and left images of the Taiwan flag, plus a rallying cry to

'Reconquer the mainland'. In all, Chinese hackers are said to have broken into – 165 times between August and September 1999 – Taiwan's Bureau of Investigation, the Ministry of Economic Affairs, the National Assembly, and the American Institute in Taiwan. Taiwanese cyberwarriors are accused of planting the 'Bloody 6/4' virus in Chinese computers as a protest against Tiananmen Square, and the Michelangelo virus that was responsible for damaging 360,000 computers throughout China. Both sides are now reconsidering their approach to information war. The *People's Daily* on 9 August 2000 described how 'Enemy forces at home and abroad are sparing no effort to use this battle front to infiltrate us.' Meanwhile, Taiwan's military fears that Chinese cyberwar would be the precursor to an invasion. The Chinese military could use computers to paralyse Taiwan's military, energy production, transport, and even the economy, making invasion much easier (*Liberty Times*, 7 August2000).[25] And in homage to Sun Tzu a shot is never fired: '… attaining one hundred victories in a hundred battles is not the pinnacle of excellence. Subjugating the enemy's army without fighting is the pinnacle of excellence'. The danger is that such propaganda will provoke hostilities to escalate to a point where a shooting war becomes real.

Notes

1. See Oliver Boyd–Barrett's stimulating chapter ('International Communication and Globalisation: Contradictions and Directions') in Mohammadi (1997) for an over-view of the kind of questions that any assessment of Globalisation must ask.
2. See R. Negrine's (1996) assessment of the way television coverage of Bosnia failed to move the British government to change its policies. He concludes that this 'illustrates the powerlessness of the media to change the policy directions of political actors immersed in other struggles and pursuing other agendas'.
3. United Nations Education, Scientific and Cultural Organisation.
4. By the 1980s, the Macbride Commission shifted the premise of UNESCO's New World Information Order from the simple 'free' to the fairer (though still empirically ambiguous) 'free and balanced' flow of information.
5. *The Economist* (19–25 August 2000) has also addressed this issue: 'The effect is to reduce income inequality between people doing similar jobs in different countries, but to increase the inequality between information workers in poor countries and their poorest compatriots.'
6. Briefly, Huntington argued that conflicts after the collapse of the Cold War system will be waged not between states or ideologies, but between 'civilisations'. We ask, how can we accept the kind of equality among civilisations that Huntington's thesis assumes? Moreover, it casts conflict with Asians as inevitable and disregards the variety of civilisations that thrive in Asia today.

7.   We follow Edward Said's definition and discussion of the concept of 'Orientalism'. See his *Orientalism: Western Conceptions of the Orient* (Penguin, London, 1995 edn.).

8.   Asian values are mainly associated with the former Prime Minister of Singapore, Lee Kuan Yew. He believes that western governments have emphasised such concepts as human rights and democracy in Asian countries over each nation's tradition and culture. Democracy can only take root in those countries that have a suitable and receptive culture and national character. Otherwise, the west is merely engaging in colonialism by imposing its values on 'different' societies. See the various speeches he made during trips to Japan in 1991 and 1992, extensively reported by the Japanese press, especially *Asahi Shimbun* (18 May 1991; 23 November 1992).

9.   Kurosawa has been identified as the influence behind such mainstream Hollywood films as *Star Wars*, *The Magnificent Seven* and *Dead Men Standing*. The important thing to note is that this is represents a *conscious and deliberate influence* with the Hollywood directors openly acknowledging their debt to this Japanese film maker.

10.   The popularity of *Judge Bao* was felt most in those countries of South East Asia with a sizeable Chinese population. It was banned in Malaysia, ostensibly because of a government ban on 'costume dramas', though popular pressure reversed this decision.

11.   Tu Weiming has referred to the existence in Taiwan of what he calls 'glocalism ... an awkward coexistence of globalism and localism'.

12.   For example see S. Serra, (1999), 'The killing of Brazilian street children and the rise of the international public sphere,' in J. Curran (ed.), *Media Organisations in Society*, London, Arnold.

13.   UNESCO tried to introduce a New World Information Order (NWIO), recognising that the expansion of communications is closely linked to economic and social development. It suggested that the UN should introduce measures to shape the way the 'North' represented the 'South', and to control the volume of news about the 'South'. The most important factor in explaining its failure is the withdrawal of the US from UNESCO in 1985 on the grounds that the NWIO was ideologically motivated. The US observed that controlling the flow of information and culture (most of it American!) would not circumvent the problem; rather the less developed countries must be encouraged to develop their own media enterprises. This demonstrates the incapacity of international organisations to resolve the basic contradictions which characterise the NWIO, ie. Identity and nationalism on the one hand, and Globalisation on the other. Its association with cultural imperialism is suggested by Schiller and Nordenstreng (1979) who said that the NWIO 'is ultimately aiming at the "decolonization" of information conditions in the developing countries, and in general advocating respect for the cultural and political sovereignty of all nations.'

14.   Pandering to the government in question is not a guarantee of securing access to their markets, as Rupert Murdoch has found to his cost. Despite deliberately avoiding upsetting Beijing and revelling in Jiang Zemin's praise, Murdoch's business empire still remains sidelined in China. See the three reports included in the *Far Eastern Economic Review*, 27 July 2000, for full details.

15.   'ASEAN Grapples with Regional Internet Rules', *The Nation*, Bangkok, 5 September 1996.

16.   'Consensus on the Need to Police the Net', *Bangkok Post*, 3 September 1996.

17. This conforms to the need to avoid generalisations. Research conducted for UNESCO in 1994 found that Eastern European audiences preferred imported programmes over those produced domestically. We suggest that this is due in part to the quality of local productions. See Sepstrup and Gooneasekara (1994). We also refer to the argument by Jeremy Tunstall (1977) that cultural imperialism is based on the incorrect assumption that high levels of American media imports in Latin America during the 1960s represented a permanent condition, rather than a transitional stage in the development of indigenous programming.

18. http://www.gio.gov.tw/info/book2000/ch_161.htm. The *Reader's Digest* produces a Taiwan edition that includes articles from the original English edition, supplemented by Chinese–language essays written specifically for readers in Taiwan. In mid–2000 *National Geographic* announced that it too would launch a Taiwan edition.

19. Though we should note that Taiwan has been under serious pressure to relax quotas on foreign movies as a pre–requisite for joining the World Trade Organisation (WTO).

20. There are potential problems with this. The *Far Eastern Economic Review* (8 June 2000) carried the following report: 'A television station is in trouble after running an imported soap opera in which one character bears the name Fatimah. ... [A] member of a group called Defenders of Islam pointed out that the Koran also has a character called Fatimah. ... Station executives pointed out that the show was from Latin America and had nothing to do with Islam. ... The Defenders ... claimed that the foreign show was a deliberate attack on them. Producers even offered to use editing facilities to change the name of the character. But the group threatened to return with even larger numbers of reinforcements. In violence–plagued Indonesia, the threat was taken seriously. Although 132 parts of the 150–part series had been broadcast ... the station abruptly cancelled the show.'

21. The article continues: 'With independent and unprejudiced media regulations and proper channels of resource distribution, publicly–run stations would be free to develop without an invisible hand pulling the strings'.

22. Association of South–East Asian Nations. Taiwan is not a member.

23. The report is available at http://www.gio.gov.tw/info/asia–pacific/media3.htm. Specific measures include: tax–breaks for foreign investors in Taiwan's media and for setting up media operations on the island; reducing import tariffs on specialised media equipment; financial assistance for new media enterprises; enhancing co–operation between the two sides of the Taiwan strait (including Macau and Kong Kong). This relaxes restrictions on the import of media products from China, Chinese media production in Taiwan, and the joint production of films and television programmes.

24. Such non–political programming is essential for effective propaganda. For further discussion of propaganda and Taiwan's international media, see Rawnsley (2000a), especially Chapter 4.

25. Military exercises in Taiwan, August 2000 demonstrated Taiwan's ability to wage computer warfare and resist viruses for the first time.

Conclusion: May You Live in Interesting Times

Chen Shui–bian's victory in the 2000 presidential election can be explained by a number of factors: voter dissatisfaction with the KMT's association with corruption; the candidacy of James Soong which split the KMT down the middle; Chen's youth and charisma compared to the KMT's outdated image and distance from the electorate; the advantage of a far superior campaign strategy than any other candidate.

However, in a fundamental sense the campaign was dominated by one crucial question: Who would voters most trust to safeguard democracy in Taiwan? The KMT tried to shift the focus of the election to national security and relations with mainland China. The party has played the so-called 'stability card' since the legalisation of multi–party politics, and has always anchored its government to the idea that it alone could deal with Beijing. Would the people of Taiwan risk their security by voting into office a candidate who represented the DPP and had, in the past, campaigned on a pro–independence platform? Such admonitions were reinforced by a series of ominous warnings from Beijing that the electorate should not vote for the 'wrong' candidate. In January 2000 the Communist leadership published a White Paper that threatened to attack if Taiwan declared independence or appeared to be postponing indefinitely dealing with the issue of reunification. China's Premier, Zhu Rongji, reinforced this strong position during his March 2000 speech to the National People's Congress in which he outlined the unspecified but terrible consequences for Taiwan if a pro–independence candidate should win the election. In 1996, such intimidation had helped Lee Teng–hui secure a 54 per cent victory in Taiwan's first presidential election by direct popular vote. Four years later the obvious threats to Taiwan's security should have propelled the KMT to victory yet again, especially when the party decided to play the faithful stability card. Recalling the (in)famous 'Daisy' advertisement of President Johnson's 1964 campaign in the United States,[1] the KMT designed a series of advertisements that depicted Taiwan's young men marching off to war, the natural consequence, the voice–over suggested, of electing Chen. The media have the power to shock and to frighten, or so the KMT clearly thought.

Chen Shui–bian's victory and the KMT's disastrous third–place showing,[2] suggest that voters in Taiwan understand the meaning of 'critical security'. For them, consolidating democracy by the peaceful transfer of political power from one party to another was more important than any threat that emanated from an increasingly 'foreign' government. Moreover, they recognise that there are other issues that are equally, if not more, important to Taiwan than cross–Strait relations and the traditional conception of 'national security'. For example, Chen's promise to stamp out political corruption was a key factor in his victory. The stunning 82 per cent turnout confirmed that voters take their national elections very seriously and consider popular participation the cornerstone of democracy. This will help protect Taiwan from 'backsliding' (Huntington, 1991) towards authoritarian politics, and will reinforce the legitimacy of the transition.

Recognising the underlying relationship between the media and democracy Chen Shui–bian's administration has moved quickly to remedy the defects in Taiwan's television industry. This is not surprising given that the DPP was for so long denied a voice in the mainstream media and has always campaigned for their de–politicisation. Chen himself had been the victim of biased news reporting many times, and expectations of what he might achieve were reinforced by his decision to make media reform a central objective of his election platform. In particular, continuing political bias has been identified as an important obstruction to the full consolidation of democracy in Taiwan. Chen promised that TTV and CTS would be transformed into genuine public television stations by increasing the government's stake in them, while CTV (funded mainly by KMT investment) would not receive a new licence once its current licence expired. The vision is commendable; the practicalities are less clear. Briefly the new government has expressed its commitment to reducing the number of shares it owns in media enterprises, and curtailing the influence in the media that political parties, government agencies and the military continue to enjoy. At the time of writing (September 2000) the provincial government still owns a major share of TTV, CTS is in the hands of the Ministry of Defense, while the KMT owns a majority share of CTV. The media, Chen said during the election campaign, should be impartial, while political parties should be prevented by new laws and regulations from using their control of the media for political and partisan purposes. However, Chen may first have to reform the GIO before he is able to tackle television, for that institution remains a conservative obstruction to radical change. The new Director–General of the GIO, Chung Chin, responded to public pressure to start the ball rolling by creating a committee of media professionals and scholars to oversee the reform process: 'Our basic aim is to filter out improper influences, both political and commercial, that may stand in the way of the neutrality of news gathering and presenting,' she told the Education and Culture Committee of the Legislative Yuan (*Taipei Times*, 2 June 2000). The committee has proposed shaking up the laws governing the ownership and listing of shares to prevent monopoly control. The plan suggests imposing mandatory listing of stocks and shares of private media, and states that government–affiliated groups should not own more than between 30 and 49 per cent of a company's total shares. However, tension has already marred proceedings: The more radical agenda of barring government, political parties and the military from owning majority shares has been shelved as too controversial and, because it may infringe the right to freedom of speech, possibly unconstitutional. Moreover, the committee wants to manage each station individually, but the GIO has made it clear that it does not want to deal in specifics. The GIO is much happier to formulate a general plan for reform, and seems to favour privatisation rather than Chen's vision of public broadcasting. This has angered media scholars who testify that privatisation will necessarily damage democracy in Taiwan: Programmes would be low quality, while the stations would be owned by only a few consortia. The solution is a genuinely public television system that emphasises quality through serious investment, and would make a major contribution to popular empowerment. However, few understand that, after forty years of control over television by the government, it is difficult to persuade people of the merit of handing control back to the government which is what, in layman's terms, public television means. They see this as a threat to democracy's survival. Taiwan's population is now committed to preserving the democratic system – witness the continuing high turnouts at elections – and they are determined to resist any hints of threats to its critical security. The dilemma facing the government's relationship with the television stations has been addressed in a thought provoking article in the *Taipei Times* by Ho Jung–hsing (of the *Liberty Times*), and Shih Shih–hao and Weng Hsiu–chi, both of National Chengchi University. 'An appropriate relationship between the government and TV stations is a complex issue,' they wrote:

> This is not just about a "retreat" from TV stations owned and controlled by the government. It is about how the government, in the broadest sense, assures the professional independence of the content broadcast on its stations. It is also about how the government is addressing the problems in an increasingly crowded market for terrestrial, satellite and cable TV stations through structural reforms (*Taipei Times*, 29 May 2000).

The writers of this passage share the same idea as many media scholars in Taiwan, including Feng Chien–shan who has launched a campaign to lobby for the creation of more public television stations. They advocate 'deprivatised ownership' and 'professional management' of TTV and CTS, that is, separating the ownership and management of both stations. The government would merely own the stations without having any management powers. The stations would be responsible for their own financing, allowing profits to be ploughed back into the production of programmes. This, they believe, would strengthen and secure Taiwan's democracy, and encourage the empowerment of a revitalised civil society. It is still far too early to assess whether their optimism is justified. Nevertheless, such opinions do confirm that the concept of 'critical security' is broadening out in terms of the issues it encompasses and the people who are now thinking about them.

At least the GIO does agree on the need for a regulatory framework that will allow journalists the freedom to carry out their work without fear of provoking the government. Particularly welcome is Chen's commitment to incorporate the International Bill of Rights into domestic law, and his promise to create an independent human rights committee (*Taipei Times*, 2 August 2000). This *should* guarantee freedom of information and communication in Taiwan, thus encouraging journalists to fulfil their designated role in the democratic process – as a check on government, and as an agency for the close scrutiny of politicians and policy on behalf of all citizens in Taiwan. The emphasis in this sentence must fall on the word 'should': In what seems like an ominous echo of previous times, members of the Taipei District Prosecutor's Office searched the offices and homes of journalists working for the *China Times Express* on 3 October 2000 for information allegedly leaked to the media on the investigation into the corruption of a high level officer in the National Security Bureau. Journalists employed by the newspaper have complained that their telephones and those of their friends and families are bugged, and that have been placed under surveillance. The prosecutors justified their action with reference to 'national security'. The information leaked, they claimed, could include 'highly sensitive state secrets' that threatened the lives of Bureau operatives (*Taipei Times*, 4 October 2000). More than at any other time in Taiwan's recent history – the election of Chen Shui–bian held out the promise that such practices would end – the events of October 2000 have highlighted the dilemmas faced by a media operating in a democracy that must still consider national security as a priority. Journalists must monitor and scrutinise the actions of government. This means there will be confrontation between the media and the government as they have different interests and follow different agendas. But whether journalists should be held responsible for leaked information is another matter altogether. The media certainly have a responsibility to verify the facts they have before them and then make a considered decision on whether to run the story or not. They must exercise discretion, aware that sometimes their decision may run counter to national security. This calls for a level of self–discipline that few of Taiwan's media have demonstrated. Commitment to the abstract notion of 'democracy' is no panacea for solving the media's problems in dealing with the state which clings to the idea that the media somehow represent a real threat to security.

Journalists have been in a very difficult position since the 2000 election, as they have found themselves having to renegotiate their relationship to the political process and realign with sometimes alien values. Newspaper reporters who previously considered themselves the mouthpiece of the political opposition are now struggling to define a role for themselves in a Chen administration: Are they still 'oppositionist', which in crude terms means being anti–Chen (and possibly pro–KMT)? Do they remain in favour of the administration regardless of the clumsy way it has handled many issues? Or is there a third 'objective' way that they have so far insufficiently explored? The problem is particularly challenging for Formosa Television Corporation (FTC), owned by DPP–affiliated shareholders, yet committed to being an 'opposition' television station. FTC has so far resisted any attempts to transform it into a station that is openly critical of the Chen administration, though future shake–ups may change its direction. Watch this space.

Media reform has attracted critical attention because of the controversy surrounding the appointment of Lai Kuo–chou, the son–in–law of former ROC President Lee Teng–hui, as chairman of TTV. Many critics[3] have viewed this as a sign that the government is not serious about reform, and that the GIO committee with responsibility for managing change either has no real powers to make recommendations of its own, or it is unwilling to upset the status quo. The burning question is: Was Lai Kuo–chou's appointment based on his familial relationship with Lee, or has his background (a PhD in journalism and experience as a producer/host of several TTV programmes) provided adequate preparation for a career as chairman of a national television station? The fog surrounding his appointment makes it difficult to reach a satisfactory conclusion. But the issue does demonstrate that politics will continue to be an unwelcome intrusion into Taiwan's media industry (the deputy minister of finance who helps oversee six major commercial banks that together own 38 percent of TTV's shares asked the shareholders to support Lai), and any attempts at extensive change will have to balance the interests of political factions, shareholders, media practitioners concerned with preserving the development of an objective, non–partisan media profession, and finally the viewing public. The TTV Labour Union has already declared its opposition to the Lai's appointment on the grounds that the station must remain free from political interference. That a media union is able to organise in Taiwan and express its disagreement with the government over its media policies is a clear indication of how far Taiwan has progressed in a relatively short time.

Many of the social movements that worked closely with the DPP before the election are now in the process of redefining their relationship with the new administration. They are hopeful, but do not expect too much given that the KMT remains the majority party in the Legislative Yuan. They expect this situation to force the DPP to sit up and take notice of them in an effort to appeal to counter the party's lack of influence in the legislature by firming up it popular support. The executive director of the voluntary Sunshine Social Welfare Foundation, established in 1981 to help victims of facial injuries and burns, summarised the feelings of all such movements: 'We really hope that the DPP will honour their campaign promises and listen to our opinions. After all, they're a weak government – what else can they do?' (*Taipei Review*, May 2000). Clearly the media will play a defining role in the expected renaissance of civil society: They will bring to the attention of the public and politicians a wide range of issues that have until now been drowned out by their concentration on cross–Strait affairs. Likewise the media will provide a voice for social movements, especially those that are critical of the government or applying pressure to meet their objectives. Chen Ma–lin, the secretary–general of the Homemaker's Union and Foundation (a social movement concerned with environmental issues) has said that Taiwan 'should closely monitor the performance' of the new President (*Taipei Review*, May 2000). That will be the easy part: The media are on hand to report it all, every minor achievement and every little slip–up. The problem is that they are unable to see the wood for the trees. Taiwan's television news programmes continue to focus on the sensational, the dramatic, and the harrowing, and fail to provide any context to the stories they cover. By providing superficial, black–and–white coverage to otherwise complex issues, especially Taiwan's relations with the PRC, the media themselves are a potential threat to critical security.

Civil society has also become increasingly concerned with the performance of the media. These social movements are less concerned with political interference, issues of ownership and complicated share allocations, than with the media's influence in society. Again, this is evidence of a reassessment of what security means in Taiwan. June 2000 saw the creation of an alliance of 'media activists' to monitor TV programmes and identify those they considered unsuitable for children. The president of the Taiwan Media Watch Foundation described the contradictions that are inherent in the media systems of modern liberal–democracies: When does freedom of speech end and moral responsibility begin? This is a dilemma that few within the television industry have tackled with any serious intention of resolving, and their lack of sensitivity in reporting disasters, crime and personal tragedies suggests that the industry is incapable of exercising professional self–discipline.

> Any government intervention in the operations of the media is unacceptable because freedom of the press is pivotal in a civilised society. But as the tendency toward indecency looms large in our local TV programming, to expect self–discipline on the part of the media is a difficult option. So the only feasible solution is to allow the public to use its voice to tell the media what they consider to be quality TV programmes (*Taipei Times*, 5 June 2000).

The president promised that the alliance would not interfere with the freedom of the press, but instead would provide a channel of communication between viewers and producers. Such a forum has been absent throughout the history of broadcasting in Taiwan, and has therefore been a serious impediment to the realisation of a fully democratic system that serves viewers first. This book has chronicled how television, like politics, has been an elite–driven activity that denied viewers any significant or genuine opportunity to air their views and opinions. In democratic Taiwan that will change. Taiwan needs more of these groups to hold the media, and especially television, responsible for their often sensationalist and sometimes outrageous news coverage. The problem is how to make such pressure sufficiently systematic and effective that the media industry will sit up and take notice. After all, the aspiration to give 'the public' a voice on media issues is noble, but do would such groups compensate for the lack of a homogenous 'public'? If there is a lack of consensus among groups on media issues, do their views cancel each other out and thus lose any effect they might otherwise have? As we have argued in this book, the public sphere is not the same as the media sphere.

Media reform in Taiwan is the subject of much speculation, debate and even anxiety. This is encouraging, for whatever the specifics of this debate, the fact that such discussion is proceeding at all is a testimony to how far Taiwan has progressed in little over a decade. The media have advanced from being either the mouthpiece of the government or the voice of an opposition movement considered subversive and a threat to national security, to occupying a central position in a market–place that promotes pluralism. Other societies have yet to experience such change, and a recent report has named Cuba, Tunisia, Yugoslavia, Peru and Malaysia as among the 'Ten Worst Enemies of the Press' (Committee to Protect Journalists, 2000). China came second in the list behind Cuba, indicating that the media have a particularly gruelling existence on the other side of the Taiwan strait. Although the Chinese government has encouraged the state media to investigate and report the endemic corruption there, journalists do not feel able to dig too deeply or find fault with either high–level cadres or with the Communist party itself. Xinhua news agency reporter Gao Qinrong has been in jail since December 1998 on charges of bribery, embezzlement and pimping. His arrest followed revelations that a major irrigation project in an area of northern China blighted by drought was a fraudulent enterprise to help local officials win promotions. Gao's report was circulated within the Communist party before it was reported in the media, including China Central Television. In August 2000 a caller to a phone–in talk show on Chinese radio said that the only cure for corruption in China was for the Communist party to step down. The head of the station in Guangdong was fired. Several days later Associated Press (AP) in Beijing reported that a Chinese television station 'dismissed its news chief, transferred an editor and fined a reporter over the inadvertent airing of footage from the 1989 Tiananmen Square pro–democracy protests' (*Taipei Times*, 12 August 2000). The offending footage was transmitted during the opening ceremony of a Macau cable television station that included a promotional video. AP noted that such scenes can be shown in Macau, but in preparation for re–broadcasting the ceremony on China's Zhuhai TV, editors failed to notice that the Tiananmen footage could be seen on the video in the background. Journalists in Hong Kong continue to test their relationship with the new government there and repeatedly invoke arguments on freedom of speech and of the press in criticising government attempts to interfere in their work. The battle–lines are drawn between the government of this Special Administrative Region and journalists who are urged 'not to cave in to pressure and censor themselves' (*Taipei Times*, 25 August 1999). Meanwhile also in August 2000 the Russian media reported that the government there was seeking to acquire control of the two main television stations that do not belong to the state. One station, ORT, is Russia's most popular and is considered among observers as avidly pro–Putin. In May 2000 its future was not in doubt as ORT recaptured its license after the government threatened to revoke it in response to its 'slanted' coverage of recent elections. In Russia the situation can change in a remarkably short time. At least ORT was not raided by the armed federal tax police, clad in camouflage and ski masks who in May 2000 raided the offices of Media–MOST, a media empire well–known for its critical attitude towards the government. President Putin of Russia faced a barrage of criticism over his failure to manage the rescue of 118 submariners trapped on the bottom of the ocean after an explosion in their craft, August 2000. Norwegian and British divers later confirmed that all the crew had died. In a move that many critics saw as an attempt to divert attention from the government's failures Putin decided to attack the Russian media as 'liars' who have been 'destroying the state for ten years'. In a thinly veiled assault on the owner of ORT, Putin said the media were 'unscrupulously trying to exploit this misfortune ... to gain political capital', and he threatened to punish such media proprietors and fight their influence (*Taipei Times*, 26 August 2000). In Iran hardliners prevented parliamentary debate on amending restrictive press laws. Reformists were branded traitors, and state–run media were prohibited from showing footage of demonstrations in support of reform, though the media defied the ban. One of the last acts of the hardliners before losing control of the Majlis in February 2000 election was to pass through a press law that formed the basis of a ban on 25 publications, most of which were pro–reform, and justified the arrest of several prominent journalists. *Bahar* was ordered closed for 'disturbing public opinion' and 'inciting unrest'. On 21 July 2000, a Serb journalist who reported on atrocities in Kosovo (and was recently named European Internet Journalist of the Year) went on trial for espionage. He was also accused of spreading false information with the intention of inciting civil unrest (*Taipei Times*, 22 July 2000). In August a an international team of journalists working for a British production company were arrested and charged with espionage in Liberia. The authorities reviewed their video footage and discovered material that was 'damaging to the Liberian government and the security of the state' (*Taipei Times*, 21 August 2000).[4] In situations of conflict, civil war or national crisis, the security of journalists remains as vulnerable as it ever was.[5] Also in July 2000, Britain's notorious *News of the World* made international headlines when it printed the names and photographs of 49 convicted paedophiles. This was a response to public outrage over the abduction and murder of an eight years–old girl. The newspaper dismissed the idea that its 'name and shame' campaign lacked moral justification. Critics accused it of inciting a lynch–mob mentality (crowds attacked an innocent man in his own home after they had 'mistaken' him for one of the named offenders), while experts claimed the paper's action would make it more difficult for the authorities to keep track of known paedophiles who would now go underground and thus put children at greater risk. The *News of the World*'s response to criticism raises important issues about moral responsibility, freedom of information and the security of both offenders and the victims. It also reveals the tabloid's reasoning in publishing the list:

> "We're convinced we're doing the right thing", executive editor Robert Warren told BBC Radio. "It's about protecting children. It's something the *News of the World* has been keen on for a long, long time and has pursued with great energy. *If it sells newspapers, so be it*" (emphasis added. *Taipei Times*, 24 June 2000).

Such incidents only conform that critical security is a complex concept, one that defies easy definition. The media's role and responsibility in helping to achieve security – of the individual, the community, the nation, the state – will continue to be the subject of national and international politics.

On 22 July 2000, President Chen faced the biggest crisis of his two–months old administration. Four river workers, three me and one women, were trapped by the surging waters of Pachang Creek in southern Taiwan. After nearly three hours waiting to be rescued the workers were swept away by raging currents. All four drowned.

The image of the four clinging to each other in desperation is an image that will forever haunt Taiwan and those who were there at the time, including the authors. For the events of 22 July were broadcast live across the island by all Taiwan's television networks. The crisis generated a media frenzy that threatened the survival of the administration: How could the government allow police and military officials argue over red–tape and whose responsibility it was to help, while viewers could only helplessly watch the four die? Photographs of the trapped workers continued to dominate the font page of newspapers into August, while official investigations, recriminations, and culpability ensured that the harrowing scenes were played again and again on the television news. The crisis represents a fundamental dilemma: Should the news media continue to show such upsetting footage merely to illustrate a point that all viewers understand anyway? Or does the repetition help to remind us of the story behind the crisis, questions about the government's responsiveness to public needs and the nature of accountability? The media failed to explore the background and context of the tragedy. For example, only the English language *Taipei Times* questioned why the workers were in the river in the first place when warnings of torrential rain had been issued. The *Taipei Times* also addressed general issues of labour safety and welfare, a dimension to the story that was absent in most media coverage of the tragedy:

> Media reports over the past three days have overwhelmingly focused on the government's responsibility in the matter, but the occupational injury victims' groups believe the accident is a reflection of long–existing shortcomings in workplace safety. ...
>
> "This is not an isolated case at all. Such things happen in Taiwan from time to time where workers die of occupational injuries. *It's just that the other cases haven't grabbed media and public attention"* ... (emphasis added. *Taipei Times*, 27 July 2000).

Meanwhile as we write these words in Taipei, the first anniversary of the devastating earthquake that hit the island on 21 September 1999 is approaching. The consequences of the earthquake have rarely been out of the media: Landslides caused by the combination of aftershocks and torrential rain have added to the damage; residents at the epicentre are still fighting for compensation and in some cases, re-housing; and the Pachang Creek tragedy has reminded all of Taiwan that governments are most vulnerable to political pressure in times of crisis. But the media themselves have also been the target of criticism. Parents and teachers have accused horror shows on television during 'Ghost Month' (the seventh month of the lunar calendar when the gates of hell supposedly open and the dead walk the earth) of frightening young viewers in those areas hardest hit by the earthquake, threatening efforts to help them overcome their trauma. In a curious confession of government powerlessness, the GIO has admitted there is little it can do given that programmes are given ratings decided by broadcasting corporations (*Taipei Times*, 11 August 2000). Is this the price to pay for 'freedom'?

Threats to security do indeed materialise in many guises.

Notes

1. This is probably the most famous campaign advertisement in political history. It depicted a small girl picking the leaves from a daisy and counting them. The picture freezes and a we hear a booming countdown from ten to one, at which point we see a nuclear explosion. Johnson's voice then implies that voters have a choice between voting for his rival, Cold War hawk Barry Goldwater and risking nuclear war, or vote for Johnson which equals a vote for peace.
2. Chen won 39.3 per cent of the vote; James Soong, the 'maverick' (as the media liked to refer to him in recognition of his expulsion from the KMT) independent candidate won 36.8 per cent; the KMT's Lien Chan gained a scant 23.1 per cent.

3. For example, Chiu Hei–yuan of Academia Sinica, and Lee Ching–an, a legislator from James Soong's new People's First Party.
4. Under mounting international pressure the Liberian government dropped all charges, but the journalists were required to apologise in return.
5. See Philip Knightley, *The First Casualty: The War Correspondent as Hero and Mythmaker from the Crimea to Kosovo*, Prion Books, London, 2000.

Bibliography

Antola, L. and Rogers, E. (1984), 'Television Flows in Latin America', *Communication Research*, Vol.11, No.2.

Arrigo, L.G. (1981), 'Social Origins of the Taiwan Democratic Movement', in *Meilitao* (Chinese), April–May.

Bagdikian, B. (1990), *The Media Monopoly*, Beacon Press, Boston.

Baum, R. (1994), *Burying Mao: Chinese Politics in the Age of Deng Xiaoping*, Princeton University Press, Princeton.

Bens, E., Kelly, M. and Bakke, M. (1992), 'Television content: Dallasification of culture?' in Siune, K. and Truetzscher, W. (eds.), *Dynamics of Media Politics*, Sage, London.

Berman, D.K. (1992), *Words Like Colored Glass: The Role of the Press in Taiwan's Democratization Process*, Westview Press, Boulder, Colorado.

Bobbio, N. (1987), *The Future of Democracy*, University of Minnesota Press, Minnesota.

Bobbio, N. (1989), *Democracy and Dictatorship: The Nature and Limits of State Power*, Polity, Oxford.

Booth, K. and Trood, R. (1999), *Strategic Culture in the Asia–Pacific*, Macmillan, London.

Borg, D. and Heinrichs, W. (1980), *Uncertain Years: Chinese–American Relations, 1947–1950*, Columbia University Press, New York.

Boyd–Barrett, O. (1997), 'International Communication and Globalization: Contradictions and Directions', in Mohammadi, A. (ed.) (1997), *International Communication and Globalization*, Sage, London.

Browne, D.R. (1989), *Comparing Broadcasting Systems: The Experiences of Six Industralized Nations*, Iowa State University Press, Iowa.

Buzan, B. (1991), *People, States and Fear: An Agenda for International Security Studies in the Post–Cold War Era*, Harvester Wheatsheaf, London.

Cahill, K.H. (ed.) (1996), *Preventive Diplomacy: Stopping Wars Before They Start*, Basic Books, New York.

Carlyle, T. (1907), *On Heroes, Hero Worship and the Heroic in History*, Chapman Hall, London.

Castells, M. (1997), *The Information Age: Economy, Society and Culture* Vol.2, *The Power of Identity*, Blackwells, Oxford.

Chalaby, J.K. (1998), *The Invention of Journalism*, Macmillan, London.

Chan, J. M. (1996), 'Television in Greater China: Structure, Exports, and Market Formation', in Sinclair, J., Jacka, E., and Cunningham, S. (eds.), *New Patterns in Global Television: Peripheral Vision*, Oxford University Press, Oxford.

Chan, J.M. (1997), 'National responses and accessibility to STAR TV in Asia', in Sreberny–Mohammadi, A., Winseck, D., McKenna, J., and Boyd-Barrett, O., (eds.) *Media in Global Context*, Arnold, London.

Chang, C.K. (1995), *From Refinement to Perfection* (Chinese), Chiu-Ke Publishing Ltd., Taipei.

Chao, L. and Myers, R.H. (1998), *The First Chinese Democracy: Political Life in the Republic of China*, Johns Hopkins University Press, Baltimore.

Chen, F.M. (ed.) (1992), *The February 28th Incident* (Chinese), Chien–Wei Publication, Taipei.

Chen, G.Y. (1982), 'The Reform Movement Among Intellectuals in Taiwan Since 1970', in *Bulletin of Concerned Asian Scholars*, Vol.13, No.3.

Chen, K.H. and Chu, P. (1987), *Forty Year Evolution of the Newspaper Industry on Taiwan*, Independence Evening News, Taipei.

Chen, M.T. (1995), *Faction Politics and Taiwan's Political Reform* (Chinese), Yueh–Tan Publishing, Taipei.

Chen, S.Y. (1998), 'State, Media and Democracy in Taiwan', *Media, Culture & Society* Vol. 20, No.1, pp. 9-29.

Cheng, J.C. *et al.* (ed) (1993), *Deconstructing Broadcasting Media: Establishing the New Order of Broadcasting Media* (Chinese) Cheng Society, Taipei.

Cheng, T.J. and Haggard, S. (eds.) (1992), *Political Change in Taiwan*, Lynne Rienner, Boulder.

Chiang, C.K. (1991), *Collected Works of Mr. Chiang Ching–kuo* (Chinese), Taipei, Government Information Office.

Chiou, C. L. (1995), *Democratizing Oriental Despotism: China from 4 May 1919 to 4June 1989 and Taiwan from 28 February 1947 to 28 June 1990*, Macmillan, London.

Chiu, H. (1993), 'Constitutional Development in the Republic of China in Taiwan', in Tsang, S. (ed.), *In the Shadow of China: Political Developments in Taiwan*, Hurst & Company, London.

Chu, Y.H. (1996), 'Taiwan's Unique Challenges', in *Journal of Democracy*, Vol.7, No.3.

Comor, E.A. (1997), 'The retooling of American hegemony: US foreign communication policy from free flow to free trade', in Sreberny–Mohammadi, A., Winseck, D., McKenna, J., and Boyd-Barrett, O., (eds.) *Media in Global Context*, Arnold, London.

Copper, J.F. (1996), *Taiwan: Nation-State or Province?* 2nd Edition, Westview Press.

Copper, J.F. (1997), *The Taiwan Political Miracle: Essays on Political Development, Elections and Foreign Relations*, University Press of America, Lanham, Maryland.

Copper, J.F. (1999), *As Taiwan Approaches the New Millennium: Essays on Politics and Foreign Affairs*, University Press of America, Lanham, Maryland.

Curran, J. and Park, M.J. (eds.) (1999), *De-westernizing Media Studies*, Routledge, London.

Dahl, Robert (1991 ed), *Poliarchy: Participation and Opposition*, Yale University Press, New Haven.

Dahlgren, P. (1995), *Television and the Public Sphere: Citizenship, Democracy and the Media*, Sage, London.

Diamond, E. and Silverman, R.A. (1995), *White House to Your House: Media and Politics in Virtual America*, MIT Press, Cambridge.

Diamond, L. and Plattner, M.F. (1998), *Democracy in East Asia*, Johns Hopkins University Press, Baltimore.

Dickson, B.J. (1997), *Democratization in China and Taiwan: The Adaptability of Leninist Parties*, Clarendon Press, Oxford.

Domes, J. (1981), 'Political Differentiation in Taiwan: Group Formation Within the Ruling Party and the Opposition Circles, 1979–1980', in *Asian Survey*, Vol.21, No.10.

Elegant, S. (1996), 'Voice of the People', in *Far Eastern Economic Review*, 16 September 1996.

Enzensberger, H.M. (1970), 'Constituents of a Theory of the Media', *New Left Review*, vol.64, pp. 13–36.

Falk, R. (1995), *On Human Governance: Toward a New Global Politics*, Polity, Cambridge.

Fang, C.S. (1995), *The Political Economy of the Broadcasting Media's Capital Movement: The Analysis of the Changes in Taiwan's Broadcasting Media*, Taipei, Taiwan: A Radical Quarterly in Social Studies.

Fang, C.S. (1998), *Big Media* (Chinese), Taipei, Meta Media.

Fei, J., Ranis, G., and Kuo, S. (1979), *Growth with Equality*, Oxford University Press, Oxford.

Ferdinand, P. (ed.) (1996), *Take-off for Taiwan?*, Royal Institute of International Affairs, London.

Gaddis, J.L. (1997), *We Now Know: Rethinking the Cold War*, Oxford University Press, Oxford.

Garnham, N. (1993), 'The Future of the BBC', in *Sight and Sound*, Vol.3, February.

Garnham, N. (1997), 'Political Economy and the Practice of Cultural Studies', in P, Golding and M. Ferguson (eds.), *Cultural Studies in Question*, Sage, London.

Gellner, E. (1995), *Encounters with Nationalism*, Polity Press, London.

Gibson, J.L. (1998), *Social Networks and Civil Society in Processes of Democratization*, Studies in Public Policy 301, Centre for the Study of Public Policy, University of Strathclyde.

Giddens, A. (1990), *The Consequences of Modernity*, Stanford University Press, Stanford.

Giddens, A. (1991), *Modernity and Self–Identity*, Polity Press, Cambridge.

Giddens, A. (1994), *Beyond Left and Right*, Polity Press, Cambridge.

Giliomee, H. and Simkins, C. (eds) (1999), *The Awkward Embrace: One–Party Domination and Democracy*, Harwood, Amsterdam.

Gill, G. (2000), *The Dynamics of Democratization: Elites, Civil Society and the Transition Process*, London: Macmillan.

Gold, T. B. (1986), *State and Society in the Taiwan Miracle*, M. E. Sharpe Inc., New York.

Gold, T. B. (1993a), 'Taiwan's Quest for Identity in the Shadow of China', in Tsang, S. (ed.), *In the Shadow of China: Political Developments in Taiwan*, Hurst & Company, London.

Gold, T. B. (1993b), 'Go With Your Feelings: Hong Kong and Popular Culture in Taiwan', *China Quarterly*, Vol.136, No.4, pp.907-925.

Government Information Office (1985), *Developing Public Television in the Future* (Chinese), Taipei, GIO.

Government Information Office (1999), *Taiwan's Media in the Democratic Era*, GIO, Taipei.

Habermas, J. (1962/1989), *Structural Transformation of the Public Sphere*, Polity Press, Cambridge.

Hall, J. (ed) (1995), *Civil Society: Theory, History, Comparison*, Polity Press, London.

Hallin, D.J. (1986), *The Uncensored War: The Media and Vietnam*.

Harrell, S. and Huang, C.C. (eds) (1994), *Cultural Change in Postwar Taiwan*, SMC Publishing, Taipei.

Holmes, S. (1990), 'Liberal Constraints on Power? Reflections on the Origins and Rationale of Access Regulation' in J. Lichtenberg (ed.), *Mass Media and Democracy*, Cambridge University Press, New York.

Hood, S.J. (1997), *The Kuomintang and the Democratization of Taiwan*, Westview Press, Boulder.

Hsieh, J.F. and Niou, M.S. (1996), 'Taiwan's March 1996 Elections', in *Electoral Studies*, Vol.15, No.4.

Hu, J. (1994), 'Freedom of Expression and Development of the Media', in J. Hu (ed), *Quiet Revolutions on Taiwan, Republic of China*, Kwang Hwa, Taipei, pp. 478–500.

Huntington, S. (1965), 'Political Development and Political Decay', in *World Politics*, Vol. 17, No.2.

Huntington, S. (1991), *The Third Wave: Democratization in the Late Twentieth Century*, University of Oklahoma Press, Norman.

Huntington, S. (1996), *The Clash of Civilizations and the Remaking of the World Order*, Simon & Schuster, New York.

Huntington, S. and Nelson, J.M. (1976), *No Easy Choice: Political Participation in Developing Countries*, Harvard University Press, London.

Hwang, J. (1996), 'Cable Cat's Cradle', in *Free China Review*, Vol.46, No.2.

Jabri, V. (1996), *Discourse on Violence: Conflict Analysis Reconsidered*, Manchester University Press, Manchester.

Karl, T.L., and Schmitter, P.C., 'Democratization Around the Globe: Opportunities and Risks, in Klare, M.T. and Thomas D.C. (eds) (1994), *World Security: Challenges for a New Century*, St. Martin's Press, New York, pp.43–62.

Keane, J. (1991), *The Media and Democracy*, Polity, Oxford.

Keane, J. (1993), 'Democracy and the Media: Without Foundations', in D. Held (ed.), *Prospects for Democracy*, Polity Press, London.

Keane, J. (1996), *Reflections on Violence*, Verso, London.

Kelley, D. and Donway, R. (1990), 'Liberalism and Free Speech', in J. Lichtenberg (ed.), *Mass Media and Democracy*, Cambridge University Press, New York.

Kerr, G.H. (1966), *Formosa Betrayed*, Eyre & Spottiswoode, London.

Klare, M.T. and Thomas D.C. (eds) (1994), *World Security: Challenges for a New Century*, St. Martin's Press, New York.

Klintworth, G. (1995), *New Taiwan, New China: Taiwan's Changing Role in the Asia–Pacific Region*, Longman, Melbourne.

Krause, K. and Williams, M.C. (eds) (1997), *Critical Security Studies*, University of Minnesota Press, Minneapolis.

Kuo, L.H. (1990), *Criticism of Television and Observation of the Media* (Chinese), China Times Publication Ltd., Taipei.

Lai, T., Myers, R. and Wei, W (1991), *A Tragic Beginning: The Taiwan Uprising of February 28, 1947*, Stanford University Press, California.

Laufer, R. and Paradeise, C. (1989), *Marketing Democracy: Public Opinion and Media Formation in Democratic Societies*, Transaction Books, Brunswick, New Jersey.

Lee, C.C. (1979), *Media Imperialism Reconsidered: The Homogenizing of Television Culture*, Sage, London.

Lee, C. C. (1989), *Media Imperialism* (in Chinese), China Times Culture Publication Ltd., Taipei.

Lee, C.C. (1992), 'Emancipated from Authoritarian Rule: The Political Economy of the Press in Taiwan', in Chu, L. and Chan, J.M. (eds.), *Mass Communication and Social Change* (Chinese), Chinese University, Hong Kong.

Lee, C.C. (1999), 'State, Capital and Media: The Case of Taiwan', in Curran, J. and Park, M.J. (eds.), *De-westernizing Media Studies*, Routledge, London.

Leonard, A. (1991), *Freedom to be Irresponsible: Taiwan Independence and the Post–Martial Law Taiwan Press*, MA Thesis, University of California at Berkeley.

Lerner, D. (1963), 'Toward a Communication Theory of Modernization', in Pye, L. (ed.), *Communications and Political Development*, Princeton University Press, Princeton.

Li, X.F. (1991), *The Forty Year Taiwan Democracy Movement* (Chinese), Zili wanbaoshe wenhua chubanbu, Taipei.

Liebes, T. and Katz, E. (1990), *The Export of Meaning: Cross-Cultural Readings of 'Dallas'*, Oxford University Press, New York.

Lipschultz, R. (ed) (1995), *On Security*, Columbia University Press, New York.

Liu, C.H. (ed) (1995), *Give Taiwan a Chance: Photographs Collection* (Chinese), Taipei, DPP Central Headquarters.

Long, S. (1991), *Taiwan: China's Last Frontier*, Macmillan, London.

McGrew, T. (1992), 'A Global Society?' in Hall, S. and McGrew, T. (eds.), *Modernity and its Futures*, Polity Press, Cambridge.

McQuail, D. (1987), *Mass Communication Theory: An Introduction*, Sage, London.

Marks, T.A. (1998), *Counterrevolution in China: Wang Sheng and the Kuomintang*, Frank Cass, London.

Mengin, F. (1999), 'State and Identity', in Tsang, S. and Tien, H. (eds.) (1999), *Democratization in Taiwan: Implications for China*, Macmillan, London.

Meskill, J. (1979), *A Chinese Pioneer Family*, Princeton University Press, Princeton.

Metraux, D. (1991), *Taiwan's Political and Economic Growth in the Late Twentieth Century*, Edwin Mellen Press, New York.

Mohammadi, A. (ed.) (1997), *International Communication and Globalization*, Sage, London.

Moody, P.R. (1995), *Tradition and Modernization in China and Japan*, Wadsworth, Belmont, CA.

Morley, D. and Robins, K. (1989), 'Spaces of Identity: Communications, technologies and the reconfiguration of Europe', *Screen*, Vol.30, No.4, pp.10–34.

Negrine, R. (1989 and 1994), *Politics and the Mass Media in Britain*, Routledge, London.

Negrine, R. (1996), *The Communication of Politics*, Sage, London.

Negrine, R. (1997), 'Communications Technologies: An Overview', in Mohammadi, A. (ed.), *International Communication and Globalization*, Sage, London.

Nie, N.H. and Verba, S. (1972), *Participation in America: Political Democracy and Social Equality*, Chicago University Press, Chicago.

Przeworski, A. (1991), *Democracy and the Market: Political and Economic Reform in Eastern Europe and Latin America*, Cambridge University Press, Cambridge.

Randall, V. (1993), 'The Media and Democratisation in the Third World', *Third World Quarterly*, vol.14, pp.625–46.

Rawnsley, G.D. (1996), *Radio Diplomacy and Propaganda: The BBC and VOA in International Politics, 1956–64*, Macmillan, London.

Rawnsley, G.D. (1997), 'The 1996 Presidential Election Campaign in Taiwan', in *The Harvard International Journal of Press/Politics*, Vol.2, No.2.

Rawnsley, G.D. (2000a), *Taiwan's Informal Diplomacy and Propaganda*, Macmillan, London.

Rawnsley, G.D. (2000b), 'Taiwan's Propaganda Cold War: The Offshore Islands Crises of 1954 and 1958', in Aldrich, J., Rawnsley, G.D., and Rawnsley, M.Y.T., *The Clandestine Cold War in Asia: Western Intelligence, Propaganda and Special Operations*, Frank Cass, London, pp.82–101.

Rawnsley, G.D. (2000c), 'Selling Taiwan: Propaganda and Diplomacy', in *Issues and Studies*, Vol.36, No.3.

Rawnsley, G.D. and Rawnsley, M.Y.T. (1998), 'Regime Transition and the Media in Taiwan', in V. Randall (ed), *Democratization and the Media*, Frank Cass, London, pp.106–124.

Rawnsley, M. (1998), *Public Service Television in Taiwan*, unpublished Ph.D thesis, Institute of Communication Studies, University of Leeds.

Reiss, H. (ed.) (1991), *Kant's Political Writings*, Cambridge University Press, Cambridge.

The Republic of China on Taiwan Today: Views from Abroad (1990), Kwang Hwa Publishing, Taipei.

Robinson, J. (1996), 'Cable Campaigning', in *Free China Review*, Vol.46, No.2.

Robinson, J. (2000), *Appraising Steps in Democratization: Taiwan Elections 1986–2000*, University of West Florida Duplicating Services, Pensacola.

Robinson, M. and White, G. (eds) (1998), *The Democratic Developmental State: Politics and Institutional Design*, Oxford University Press, Oxford.

Sartori, G. (1976), *Parties and Party Systems: A Framework for Analysis*, Cambridge University Press, Cambridge.

Scannel, P. (1989), 'Public service broadcasting and modern public life', *Media Culture and Society*, vol.11, pp.135–66.

Schiller, H.I. (1969), *Mass Communications and the American Empire*, Augustus M. Kelly, New York.

Schiller, H.I. (1989), 'Striving for Communication Dominance', in Thissu, D. (ed.), *Electronic Empires*, Arnold, London.

Schiller, H.I. and Nordenstreng, K. (1979), *National Sovereignty and International Communication: A Reader*, Ablex, New Jersey.

Schumpeter, J. (1976), *Capitalism, Socialism and Democracy* (5th edn.), Allen and Unwin, London.

Sepstrup, P. and Goonesekera, A. (1994), *Television Transnationalization: Europe and Asia*, Reports and Papers, No.109, Paris, UNESCO.

Shiau, C.J. (1999), 'Civil Society and Democratization', in Tsang, S. and Tien, H. (eds.), *Democratization in Taiwan: Implications for China*, Macmillan, London.

Siebert, F., Peterson, T. and Schramm, W. (1956), *Four Theories of the Press*, University of Illinois Press, Urbana.

Splichal, S. (1994), *Media Beyond Socialism: Theory and Practice in Eastern Europe*, Westview Press, Boulder, Colorado.

Sreberny, A. (2000), 'Television, gender and democratization in the Middle East', in Curran, J. and Park, M. (eds.), *De–Westernizing Media Studies*, Routledge, London.

Sreberny–Mohammadi, A. (1996), 'Globalization, Communication and Transnational Civil Society', in Braman, S. and Sreberny–Mohammadi, A. (eds.), *Globalization, Communication and Transnational Civil Society*, Hampton Press, Cresskill.

Sreberny–Mohammadi, A., Winseck, D., Mckenna, J. and Boyd–Barrett (eds) (1997), *Media in Global Context*, Arnold, London.

Stecklow, S. (1993), 'Cyberspace clash: computer users battle high–tech marketeers over soul of Internet', *Wall Street Journal*, 16 September.

Stepp, C. (1990), 'Access in a Post–Responsibility Age', in J. Lichtenberg (ed.), *Mass Media and Democracy*, Cambridge University Press, New York.

Straubhaar, J.D. (1997), 'Distinguishing the global, regional and national levels of world television', in Sreberny–Mohammadi, A., Winseck, D., McKenna, J., and Boyd-Barrett, O., (eds.) *Media in Global Context*, Arnold, London.

Su, H. (1993), 'Language Mandarin/Dialect Policies', in Cheng, J.C. *et al.* (eds) *Deconstructing Broadcasting Media: Establishing the New Order of Broadcasting Media* (Chinese), Cheng Society, Taipei.

T'ang, K.H. (1979), 'The Obstructions and Path to Solution of Current Political Problems', in *Tsung–ho yue–k'an*, No.129.

Taylor, P.M. (1992), *War and the Media: Propaganda and Persuasion in the Gulf War*, Manchester University Press, Manchester.

Taylor, P.M. (1997), *Global Communications, International Affairs and the Media Since 1945*, Routledge, London.

Teng, S. (1997), 'Hard Pressed Taiwan's Newspapers Battle for Readers', in *Sinorama*, August.

Thompson, J. B. (1993), *The Media and Modernity: A Social Theory of the Media*, Polity Press, London.

Tien, H. (1989), *The Great Transition: Political and Social Change in the Republic of China*, SMC Publishing Inc., Taipei.

Tracey, M. (1988), 'Popular Culture and the Economics of Global Television', *Intermedia*, Vol.16, No.2.

Tsang, S. (ed) (1993), *In the Shadow of China: Political Developments in Taiwan Since 1949*, C. Hurst & Co. (Publishers) Ltd., London.

Tsang, S. and Tien, H. (eds.) (1999), *Democratization in Taiwan: Implications for China*, Macmillan, London.

Tu, W. (1996). 'Cultural Identity and the Politics of Recognition in Contemporary Taiwan', *China Quarterly*, Vol.148, No.4, pp.1115–1140.

Tun, C. *et.al.* (1992), *Voice from the Edge: The Media Against the Mainstream Visual Images and the Record of Social Movement* (Chinese), Tang–Shan Publishing, Taipei.

Tunstall, J. (1977), *The Media are American*, Constable, London.

Tunstall, J. and Palmer, M. (1981), *Media Moguls*, Routledge, London.

Veljanovski, C. (1989), 'Competition in Broadcasting' in C. Veljanovski (ed.), *Freedom in Broadcasting*, Institute of Economic Affairs, London.

Vergkese, B.G. (1996), 'Freedom of Expression', *Media Asia* Vol.23, No.3.

Wang, C.H. (1993), 'The Control of Broadcasting Media', in Cheng, J.C. (ed.), *Deconstructing Broadcasting Media: Establishing the New Order of Broadcasting Media* (Chinese), Cheng Society, Taipei.

Wasko, J. and Mosco, V. (eds) (1992), *Democratic Communications in the Information Age*, Norwood, Ablex.

Watson, J. (ed.) (1997), *Golden Arches East: McDonalds in East Asia*, Stanford University Press, Stanford.

Weng, S.C. and Sun, H.h. (1994), 'How Media Use Influences Voters' Political Knowledge, Party Preferences and their Voting Behaviour in Taiwan's 1993 General Voting', in *Journal of Electoral Studies* (Chinese), Vol.1, No.2.

Wiarda, H.J. (ed) (1985), *New Directions in Comparative Politics*, Westview Press, Boulder, Colorado.

Wu, J.J. (1995), *Taiwan's Democratization: Forces Behind the New Momentum*, Oxford University Press, Hong Kong.

Index